A Bible Study by
Barbara L. Roose

Beautiful
Already

Reclaiming God's
Perspective on Beauty

Abingdon Press / Nashville

Beautiful Already
Reclaiming God's Perspective on Beauty

This book is printed on elemental chlorine-free paper.
ISBN 978-1-5018-1354-2

16 17 18 19 20 21 22 23 24 25 — 10 9 8 7 6 5 4 3 2 1
MANUFACTURED IN THE UNITED STATES OF AMERICA

Contents

About the Author

Barbara L. Roose is a popular speaker and author who is passionate about connecting women to one another and to God, helping them apply the truths of God's Word to the practical realities and challenges they face as women in today's culture. Previously Barb was Executive Director of Ministry at CedarCreek Church in Perrysburg, Ohio, where she served on staff for fourteen years and co-led the annual Fabulous Women's Conference that reached more than 10,000 women over five years. In addition to continuing as a member of the CedarCreek teaching team, Barb is a frequent speaker at women's conferences and other events. God has shaped her heart to reach out to women who either do not know or have forgotten that they are beautiful because God created them. Her desire is for every woman to realize that she has a God-given purpose and that nothing she sees in the mirror should hold her back from fulfilling that purpose. She lives in Toledo, Ohio, with her husband, Matt. They are the proud parents of three beautiful daughters, two dogs, and a grumpy rabbit named Pal.

Follow Barbara:
Twitter   @barbroose
Instagram   @barbroose
Facebook   Facebook.com/shapestylesoul
Blog   BarbRoose.com (check here for event dates and booking information)

Introduction

One of the first things we do as women each morning is look in the mirror. The words that we use to describe what we see and how we *feel* about what we see are important. When we think to ourselves or whisper out loud, "I'm so fat" or "My nose has a hump like a camel," those words scream a loud message: *I am not enough*. This dissatisfaction and discontent that plagues us—regardless of our shape, size, and description—is compounded by our culture's unrealistic images and expectations that continually bombard us. We're left feeling discouraged.

As women, the concept of beauty involves our size, shape, style, and soul. When we experience dissatisfaction with what we see in the mirror in these areas, this is what I refer to as our *ugly struggle with beauty*. My observation is that none of us is exempt from this struggle. In one way or another, we all experience it.

Our ugly struggle with beauty isn't just about how we look; it impacts how we think and live. This struggle negatively affects not only our self-image and self-esteem but also our relationships with God and others. What is the answer? We desperately need to reclaim God's perspective on beauty, rather than allow our culture to define beauty for us.

It's tempting for us to put all of the blame on the media or beauty industry for overexposing us to vast displays of digitally altered photos or magazine headlines promising to help us drop ten pounds this week. While the images of digitized, flawless, two-dimensional bodies that fill our news feeds do have a significant impact, are they fully to blame for how we feel about ourselves? I believe that while they exacerbate our self-made drama, they aren't the only cause of our discontent and our struggle with beauty.

Who gave you the idea that you aren't beautiful? Perhaps it was a boy on the playground who teased you about your skinny legs. Did an aunt or grandma comment that you were flat-chested just like your mother? Maybe your father was too busy to tell you that you were beautiful. In any case, these messages about how we look sink into our hearts and minds, impacting how we think and feel.

As Christian women, we often avoid this beauty-related dialogue altogether. Many of us may think to ourselves, *Talking about physical beauty issues isn't very spiritual*. We roll our eyes and dismiss the need to talk about the impact of beauty-related issues on our souls. For some reason, we've deemed it unspiritual to talk about beauty. Yet we harbor all kinds of secret language, meaning that we have looks and nods that convey our opinions about how we look or feel, but we don't or won't use words to express them. There's the look we give ourselves in the mirror when we've eaten too much or the grimace that we utter when we've gotten dressed and still hate how we look. When we're alone, that secret language speaks into our hearts and minds, even though we never utter a word.

Too often we point out that God looks at the heart, but we downplay or deny that God really cares about our bodies and beauty. And when we do talk about beauty, our dialogue is often guarded. So many of us carry around metaphorical suitcases of beauty-related pain—wounds inflicted by others related to our size, shape, or style. These suitcases of memories are shackled to our hearts and minds and drag us down whenever we look into the mirror.

During this six-week Bible study, we will unpack our beliefs or experiences related to beauty that are holding us hostage. Together we will explore God's truth about beauty throughout the Scriptures, digging into passages in both the Old and New Testaments and discovering how to practically apply their truths in our lives. This discipleship-focused study is a progression that will lead us away from over-focusing on unrealistic expectations and perceived flaws toward embracing God's viewpoint of our hearts, minds, bodies, and souls. As we embark on this journey, we will

- be set free from the trap of comparison and self-ridicule,
- learn to live fully as the unique and beautiful creations God designed us to be,
- become comfortable in our own skin, and
- reach beyond ourselves to encourage and support other women.

The overarching goal is for us to see the goodness, blessing, and purpose for our bodies. Achieving this goal will equip us to "win" in the struggle against discontent and comparison and in our relationships with God and others. You'll know that you are well on your way to victory when you no longer criticize your size, shape, or style and become an encourager or mentor to other women, pointing them toward victory over their own ugly struggle with beauty.

Getting Started

For each week of our study you'll find a thematic overview and Scripture memory verse, followed by five days of homework. Each day of homework includes the following:

Beauty Mark	a key idea
Beauty Regimen	a lesson with space for recording answers and reflections (boldface pink type indicates write-in-the-book responses)
Live It Out	questions for personal application
Talk with God	suggestions for a personal time of prayer

In the margin you'll find some Extra Insights, Scripture verses, and key highlights. You will be able to complete each lesson in about twenty to thirty minutes.

These lessons will help to prepare you for the discussion and activities of the weekly group session, where you will gather with your group to watch a video and discuss what you are learning together. As you share with one another, you will learn and grow even more and be able to support one another through encouragement, accountability, and prayer.

My prayer is that God will surround you with a supportive community of women as you make this powerful journey over the next six weeks. I pray that you will have the courage to "mount up" and ride into your struggle, knowing not only that God will be with you every step of the way but also that you will be victorious!

By the end of this experience, I pray that you will be able to stand and confidently proclaim, *"I am beautiful already, inside and out. In God's eyes, I am enough just as I am!"*

Barb

Week 1

ALL ABOARD THE STRUGGLE BUS

Memory Verse

"The Lord doesn't see things the way you see them. People judge by outward appearance, but the Lord looks at the heart." (1 Samuel 16:7)

This Week's Theme
Where there is shame, we will struggle to find beauty.

I don't know about you, but facing myself in the bathroom mirror first thing in the morning is a challenging way to start the day. After spending six to eight hours in a blissful semiconsciousness, my face and body need time and a shower to "come alive" again. The first glance in the mirror is a rough sight to take in. Seriously, sometimes I wonder if I got into a fistfight overnight! I survey my wild hair, droopy eyes, and flat expression. Though I know that thirty minutes and a shower will make a huge difference, that first glance causes me to ask questions that are really quiet fears:

- Can cellulite spread overnight?
- Is that a new wrinkle?
- What's that flapping under my arms?
- Does so-and-so look this bad in the morning?

I wish that I could say those questions wash down the drain once I take my morning shower. Not really. Those questions are the offspring of two larger questions that I've grappled with over a lifetime—questions that I believe confront all women at every age and stage of life:

- Am I beautiful already?
- Am I enough?

Even if you aren't into hair, nails, clothes, or shoes, you've probably been challenged by these questions at one time or another. The inability to say yes to these two questions reflects our ugly struggle with beauty. This struggle isn't about how we look; it's about how we think and live in response to our perception of beauty. We desperately need to regain God's perspective on beauty!

This week we embark on a journey to be free of our ugly struggle with beauty. It's time we learn to live at peace with our bodies. In order to do this, we need to start at the beginning. How did the struggle begin? Why do we struggle to believe that we are beautiful already and beautiful enough just as God made us? Are you ready to get started?

Day 1: How Our Struggle Began

Beauty Mark

We all struggle with beauty.

Beauty Regimen

If we're going to investigate the origins of our ugly struggle with beauty, then we've got to go all the way back to the beginning and talk about Eve.

Do you ever think about Eve? I do. When I think about her first moments of life and the instant awareness she had of her surroundings, I wonder if she thought, *What's going on here?* Surely Eve must have noticed the beautiful, colorful flowers and trees—perhaps even a lion or tiger or other animal. My guess is that Adam was awake and excited as Eve stood and approached him, and I imagine he winked at her!

I've wondered what Eve thought the first time she looked down at her body. Did she wonder, *What's all this?* Did she know if she was a pear or apple shape? Here's one that we all want to know: Did Eve have cellulite? (Personally, I think cellulite is a consequence of the Fall!)

Once Eve got a gander at her arms, legs, stomach, thighs, and feet, I wonder what she thought. Since we know that there was perfection in the garden of Eden, we can be sure that she was content. Eve enjoyed a life of pure innocence, unmarred by any negative thoughts that we struggle with today.

If I had been Eve, I think I might have planted myself by a crystal-blue pond and gazed at my reflection all day long, repeating my own version of the oft-repeated phrase in Genesis 1: "It's all good."

We find the details of Eve's beginnings in Genesis 2. God observed Adam's loneliness and gave Adam the task of naming all the animals. In this exercise, Adam would have noticed the male and female animal pairings. It was after this that God put Adam to sleep and created Eve.

Read Genesis 2:18-23. What did Adam exclaim when God brought Eve to him?

Have you ever wondered what Eve thought about herself? Put yourself in her place and write some words that she might have used to describe how she felt about herself:

While we don't know if Eve's body was a size 0 or plus-size, we do know that she didn't have any of the beauty-related issues that we experience today over our size, shape, or style. As I mentioned in the Introduction, I call our beauty-related challenges our ugly struggle with beauty. This struggle is captured by our sighs and moans in front of the mirror when we look at ourselves and don't feel that we are good enough as we are. At first, Eve didn't experience that kind of struggle. For her, there were no sighs, moans, or groans—only peace and contentment. Can you imagine that?

There are lots of words that describe our ugly struggle with beauty, but the Bible gives us a single word in Genesis 2:25. Interestingly enough, it's a word that is introduced before it ever becomes a part of the human experience.

Read Genesis 2:25 in the margin. Even though Adam and Eve were naked, what didn't they experience?

Now the man and his wife were both naked, but they felt no shame. (Genesis 2:25)

Don't miss the significance of the phrase "felt no shame." This is the only point in human history when people walked the earth without the feelings of insecurity, guilt, or self-hatred.

Adam and Eve lived in pure innocence, not knowing good or evil. There was not one ounce of guilt-induced shame—not in their hearts, minds, bodies, or souls.[1]

Genesis 3 captures our loss of authenticity or vulnerability and the beginning of our ugly struggle with beauty. We see that Eve acted on the serpent's suggestion that the fruit would bring enlightenment. She listened to the serpent, and she was deceived into thinking that she deserved access to the same knowledge and wisdom that God has. So she ate of the fruit and gave some to Adam, and he ate too.

Read Genesis 3:7 in the margin. What happened after they ate of the fruit?

At that moment their eyes were opened, and they suddenly felt shame at their nakedness. So they sewed fig leaves together to cover themselves. (Genesis 3:7)

In that awful moment when they disobeyed God and ate of the forbidden fruit, they became aware of their rebellion against God and lost the joy of living in paradise. As innocence was stripped away, they found themselves in a nightmare of shame. I've always found it interesting that when Eve became aware of good and evil, the first thing that she did was scamper to cover her naked body.

Extra Insight:

Shame statement examples:

"I let myself go. What's wrong with me? I'm so ashamed of myself."

"Shame on me for eating dessert. I'm going to gain weight if I keep eating like this."

Imagine how horrible that moment must have been. In an instant, her once-beloved body became the source of her shame. How painful it must have been for God to observe Adam and Eve rush to create coverings to conceal the bodies He had lovingly created.

In the absence of innocence, shame and judgment have a door to enter. Ever since the Fall, we human beings have struggled with shame as we have made judgments about our bodies and physical appearance.

Circle all of the "places" where you make judgments and feel uncomfortable about your body. Though you may be tempted to circle the entire body, try to identify specific "places" or categories.

What is a shame statement you have thought or spoken aloud recently about your body or appearance?

What impact do these struggles have on how you connect with or relate to others?

In addition to judging our own bodies, we also struggle with judging the outward appearance of others. A story in the Old Testament gives us valuable insight related to this struggle.

God chose Saul to be the first king of Israel. When we're introduced to Saul in 1 Samuel 9, we find out that he was one of the tallest and most handsome guys around. But it wasn't long before people stopped talking about Saul's good looks. Why? Because Saul had a heart problem.

God called the prophet Samuel to look for a new king of Israel. Yet before Samuel began to review potential candidates, God told him what to prioritize. God's insight provides some important information about our human behavior when it comes to judging the outward appearance of others.

Read 1 Samuel 16:7 in the margin. What did God tell Samuel about how we judge outward appearance versus how God judges us?

Following God's instructions, Samuel chose Jesse's son, David, to be the next king of Israel. Though we are given information about David's appearance, we also learn something more important about David.

Read 1 Samuel 16:12 and Acts 13:22 in the margin. What do you learn about David in these verses?

When God created humanity, He wove uniqueness into our DNA. Think about this: God could have created everyone the same. He could have given us the same height, weight, shape, eye color, skin color, personality, and temperament. But He didn't. God wove diversity into our physical DNA; and as a result, we're all different colors, sizes, and shapes. Uniqueness was God's gift to us. You are unique. There is no one else like you. Uniqueness is God's gift to *you*.

Yet we tend to use our individual uniqueness as a measuring stick. We look at one another and make judgments based on what we see. We do it both secretly and openly. Remember when blond jokes were popular? Most blonds that I know weren't laughing.

Growing up, I was a tall, African American kid. Everyone assumed that I played basketball. Okay, so I did. But it bothered me that everyone made that assumption based on what they saw. Sure, I was tall, but there was more to me than just my height.

Look at 1 Samuel 16:7 again. Ponder this phrase: "People judge by outward appearance." What are some of the ways that you've

But the LORD said to Samuel, "Don't judge by his appearance or height, for I have rejected him. The LORD doesn't see things the way you see them. People judge by outward appearance, but the LORD looks at the heart." (1 Samuel 16:7)

So Jesse sent for him. He was dark and handsome, with beautiful eyes. And the LORD said, "This is the one; anoint him." (1 Samuel 16:12)

"But God removed Saul and replaced him with David, a man about whom God said, 'I have found David son of Jesse, a man after my own heart. He will do everything I want him to do.'" (Acts 13:22)

been judged by your appearance? (You can include both positive and negative responses.)

Now here's a tough question: What do you tend to evaluate regarding other women? Circle all that apply:

Hair style	Body shape	Clothing style
Weight	Nails	Shoes
Eyebrows	Purse	Skin color
Facial features	Fitness level	Dietary choices

Here's the thing: we have eyes to notice ourselves and one another. The physical act of being able to see with our eyes comes as a result of God's design. What we see with our eye is interpreted by our brain, and that's what we call vision.[3]

Practically speaking, when you look in the mirror at yourself, your eyes take in your body's features. However, it's what happens in your brain that creates images and messages that you judge to be good, bad, or otherwise.

Our goal during this study is to develop a vision—a mental picture—of ourselves that is consistent with the way God sees us. We also will discover how we can share and apply that vision in the ways we connect with others. As we learn to let go of shame, judgment, and comparison and reclaim God's divine perspective on beauty, we will begin to live fully as the unique creations God designed us to be!

Live It Out

1. What is one thing that God impressed upon your heart during today's study?

2. Do you have a sense or leading from God about what you need to think or do differently as a result of what you've studied?

Talk with God

How are you feeling at the end of today's study? What are you thinking about? Whatever your thoughts may be, take a few moments and talk with God about what you've read as well as what you are hoping God will do in your heart, mind, and life through this study.

Day 2: Beauty Narratives— What's Your Beauty Story?

Beauty Mark

The stories that we tell ourselves about beauty have a profound impact on our lives.

Beauty Regimen

> I'll never forget the day when a woman came up to me and said, No, you could never be on a magazine cover. Your face features don't work; your eyes are small, you have a small face but a big nose. I was only 14, and I had never noticed any of that stuff, you know?[4]

These are the words of supermodel Gisele Bündchen. It's hard to believe that anyone could have ever said anything negative about her face or body. However, even Gisele is not immune to the inner struggle regarding beauty that we all experience. Look at her words above and notice how her quote begins with the phrase: "I'll never forget…"

Think about the defining moments you've experienced in your family of origin, at school, or in the workplace. Do you have a defining moment? How many of those defining moments shaped your relationship with inner or outer beauty? Those experiences are all part of what I call your "beauty narrative."

A narrative is a storyline or sequences of events—related or unrelated— that form a story. When you return home from a great vacation and tell people about it, you are sharing a narrative. You are sharing a sequence of events that may or may not be interrelated, but those events are all part of your narrative. Narratives aren't about whether or not something is true, but they do contain your memories and your perspective of the events at the time.

Here are a few beauty narratives women shared with me in a survey I conducted a couple of years ago called *Created with Curves*, in which more than five hundred women from around the world answered questions about beauty:

"You're so ugly that…"
"Pretty girls like you can have anything that they want."
"Fatty, fatty, two-by-four, can't get through the kitchen door."
"Since you're so pretty, you don't have to worry about being smart."

Some of you have heard these narratives and others. Our beauty narratives are a mixture of positive and negative events, circumstances, and comments. Here's some insight into my childhood beauty narrative:

Once upon a time, there was a little girl named Barbara Louise. Young Barbara loved to ride her pink bike (with a banana seat) up and down the sidewalk and watch cartoons. Most of all, Barbara loved to gather with her favorite girl cousins to play with their dolls. Each afternoon, the girls gathered to travel into a magical dreamland with the most perfect doll of them all—Barbie.

When I was a child, Barbie dolls were everywhere. We didn't realize that Barbie's anatomical shape was unrealistic. We just loved the fact that she had great dresses with Velcro and super cute plastic shoes. Sure, sometimes our moms threatened to throw all of those shoes away because they were tired of stepping on them, but we played on!

We dreamed that Barbie could do anything. She always had a high-paying job, a great house, and an amazing sports car. In our eyes, Barbie was beautiful and perfect, and therefore anything was possible for Barbie.

I studied Barbie on a regular basis. I shared a name with the perfect doll, and I didn't look anything like her. I was a shy, skinny, little brown-skinned girl with big, thick glasses and two very large front teeth. I didn't look or feel like a Barbie, even though we shared the same name. In my little girl brain, I hoped that I could be many things when I grew up, but I never thought that being beautiful could be one of them. So, here's another piece of my beauty narrative:

Since I do not look like the pretty Barbie dolls, then I cannot be pretty. If I am not pretty, then I should not dream of all of the things that pretty little girls dream about.

Every woman has a beauty narrative. Your beauty narrative has been shaped by events throughout your lifetime, even those that are happening now! Most of our beauty narratives, particularly the painful ones, remain hidden in our hearts and minds until we have a safe place to share those stories. Sticks and stones can break our bones, and names—especially hurtful, malicious names—can stick in our minds forever. Yet when we acknowledge our narratives and place them before God, He gives us a new storyline. No matter the early chapters of your life story, God's narrative for your life includes beauty and purpose.

Today we're going to uncover our beauty narratives. This may require you to come face-to-face with some powerful and painful memories that you buried long ago although they still impact your life today.

Let's begin with our names. We know that names are powerful. Expectant parents spend quality time thinking through the name they will give to their new son or daughter. You might have been named after a family member or favorite memory. Whatever your name, your parents likely chose a moniker that in some way affirmed the kind of personality, character, or life they dreamed you might have.

Have you ever looked up the meaning of your name? My name, Barbara, is a Latin name derived from *barbarous*, meaning foreign or strange.[5] Of course, that definition leaves a lot to be desired, so I checked UrbanDictionary.com, a crowd-sourced online dictionary that allows people to assign value to names based on their personal experience or opinion. I discovered that although my name still was defined as meaning "strange," people had added adjectives and other descriptive statements such as these:

> [Barbara is] a sensitive girl who doesn't get mad easily.
> Barbara is the best girl you will ever run into.
> Barbara is beautiful, kind and funny.[6]

Isn't it interesting how people assign meanings to names?

What is your given name? What does it mean? (If you don't know, look it up online. For fun, look it up on UrbanDictionary.com too.)

What people call us sticks with us. While our parents may put a name on our birth certificate, that isn't the only name we receive in life. Most of us also have one or more nicknames given to us by family, friends, or sometimes bullies and enemies. As a result of others' perceptions, we often end up with new names, such as Dimples or Four-eyes. But it's the meanings behind those names that fill in our beauty narratives.

What are some of the nicknames you've been given through life?

What happens when our names or nicknames aren't desirable and we can't get away from them? How do those names impact our self-images, our attitudes, or our lifestyles? Are we stuck with the name someone calls us and the painful narrative that name creates?

In the Old Testament we meet a woman named Rahab who was stuck with an undesirable "name." The scriptural author introduces her as "Rahab the prostitute." Though we do not know a lot about her family of origin or ancestry, the word *prostitute* fills in a lot of blanks.

Read Joshua 2:1. As you are introduced to Rahab in this verse, what ideas and opinions about who she is and what she values come to mind?

Describe the kind of life, behaviors, or social standing that Rahab the prostitute might have experienced.

Our human nature is to put people into categories by giving them names or labels. It's a way for us to manage our beliefs and expectations when it comes to dealing with people. Imagine some of the names that the people of Jericho used to describe Rahab the prostitute: *immoral, loose, dirty,* or *shameful.* Those names became a part of Rahab's story or narrative about her life. That narrative would begin running in her mind first thing in the morning when she awakened and would replay all day long.

The same is true for us. Too often we allow our worst names to define how we see ourselves or how we live.

Jennifer, the chubby one
Big-boned Brenda
Elise, with the perfect body
Sarah, the ugly divorcée

Look back at the nicknames you listed. In the space below, list only the *undesirable* nicknames or labels that you've been called in life.

What are the negative names or labels that you've called yourself lately?

How have these names impacted how you care for yourself, make decisions, or connect with others? Is there an experience or event that you've opted out of as a result?

During my teen years, I didn't date much. In my mind I justified my lack of dates because I had buckteeth, I was too tall, and my thick-lensed glasses were a definite turnoff. Since I couldn't do anything about my teeth or being tall, I decided that I would concentrate on being "the smart one." That was a label that others gave me that I embraced.

Since people complimented me for being smart, I leaned into those compliments whenever prom or homecoming came around. I fought off the "I'll never get a date" narrative, choosing instead to embrace the "I'm too busy with homework to go" story. Yet deep inside I wanted just one nice boy to ask me to be his date. In fact, my family still hears about the fact that I was never asked to prom. While I can tell the story now with a smile, that narrative is part of my life and how I remember myself growing up.

While Rahab the prostitute might have been scorned and ridiculed because of what she did, there was so much more to her than just her name or label. In the following passage of Scripture, we find out so much more about Rahab and how God impacted her life.

Read Joshua 2:8-11. What do we learn about Rahab the prostitute in these verses?

In verse 11, what was Rahab's declaration regarding what she believed about God?

After declaring what she believed about God, Rahab boldly asked for her life as well as the lives of her family to be spared when the Israelites invaded Jericho. I love this part of Rahab's story because it would be easy to imagine that a woman demeaned as often as Rahab was would be too shy or fearful to make such a bold request. Yet Rahab's faith in God's power seemed to fuel her resolve to save her life and the lives of those whom she loved.

In Joshua 6, we read about how the Israelite army marched silently around Jericho once a day for six days. Think about how terrifying it must have been for Rahab to wait in a city filled with fearful anticipation of the unknown.

On the seventh day, the Israelite army marched around the great wall of Jericho seven times. Then the Israelites shouted and the wall came tumbling down! The Israelite army rushed into Jericho and conquered the city, killing the inhabitants inside. Yet Rahab's story has a happy ending.

Read Joshua 6:25 in the margin. Why were Rahab and her family spared?

Where did Rahab end up living?

After the fall of Jericho, Rahab's narrative is far from over! In Matthew 1, the Bible records Jesus' genealogy, and we see Rahab's name among those who are in the lineage of Christ. Imagine how stunned she would have been to know that she would be one of Jesus' ancestors. Not bad for a woman having a less-than-desirable occupation attached to her name.

Look up Matthew 1:5-7. Whom did Rahab marry?

What was her son's name?

How was Rahab the prostitute related to King David and King Solomon?

Hebrews 11 is known as the "Hall of Faith." This inspiring chapter contains the stories of named and unnamed individuals who displayed great faith, and Rahab the prostitute is listed in this esteemed group.

Read Hebrews 11:31. Why did Rahab end up being recorded in one of the most prestigious chapters in the Bible? How is she described?

At the end of your life, someone will write an obituary and your life story will be told in a limited amount of space. How would you like to be remembered? Complete the following legacy statement:

It was by faith that _____
                              (your name)

_____.

There is one more mention of Rahab the prostitute in the New Testament. For a woman who started out with such a negative narrative, she becomes a powerful example for all of us. In fact, the writer of the Book of James uses Rahab's example to show us what faith-in-action looks like.

Read James 2:25-26 in the margin. Verse 26 is an oft-repeated Scripture, but much less attention is given to verse 25. How was Rahab's life an example of faith in action?

Why do you think Rahab is identified here as "Rahab the prostitute"? What significance could that have for us?

> [25] Rahab the prostitute is another example. She was shown to be right with God by her actions when she hid those messengers and sent them safely away by a different road. [26] Just as the body is dead without breath, so also faith is dead without good works. (James 2:25-26)

A beauty narrative
is the story we
create about
our experiences
with beauty.

Although the early chapters of Rahab's narrative pointed in a certain direction, God stepped in and shifted her narrative in a new direction. Through her life, God shows us that it doesn't matter where we come from or the names that we've been given or the narratives that have shaped our lives. What matters is the faith and trust that we have in God's almighty power and sovereignty.

Whatever your beauty narrative may be, God has created a new narrative for you—a storyline in which you are treasured and valued for who He has created you to be.

Today I shared a portion of my beauty narrative. As we close, take a moment to write your own beauty narrative.

As the diagram below shows, your beauty narrative includes feelings, events, and memories that have influenced your shape (how you think and feel about your body), your style (the ways you express yourself), and your soul (the inner part of who you are).

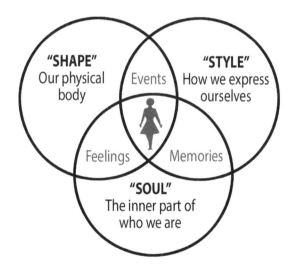

My beauty narrative (if more space is needed, additional narrative pages have been provided on pages 203-205):

How do you feel about your beauty narrative? Describe how it has impacted your life:

Do you believe that God can write a new narrative for you as He did for Rahab, resulting in a lasting legacy? Why or why not?

Review the legacy statement you completed earlier (page 21). In order for what you wrote to be true, what do you need to allow God to do in your life?

Live It Out

1. What is one thing that God impressed upon your heart during today's study?

2. Do you have a sense or leading from God about what you need to think or do differently as a result of what you've studied?

Talk with God

Dear friend, God cares about your struggle to see yourself as beautiful. Your struggle isn't trite or insignificant. If you are riding the struggle bus and heading toward an ugly ending, you can hop off that bus—if you're ready. God wants to hear from you today. Just talk to Him.

Day 3: The Land of Shame

Beauty Mark

We don't have to live in shame. We can be freed by God's truth!

Beauty Regimen

In our first lesson this week, we talked about shame's entrance into the world as a result of Adam and Eve's sin and the shameful statements we think and make about ourselves when we look into the mirror. Yesterday we considered how others contribute to our shame through undesirable names and labels, creating hurtful beauty narratives that we carry with us through life. The common denominator is shame. When it comes to our ugly struggle with beauty, shame is one of the most destructive weapons Satan uses, and secrecy increases its effectiveness. Today we will explore how we can overcome and break free from the shame that causes us to feel we are less than the women God has created us to be.

In Luke 15:11-31, Jesus tells the story of the Prodigal Son. This multi-layered story features a young man, his loving father, and his elder brother. Though most of us are familiar with the story, let's remember the storyline together.

While speaking to a group of followers and religious leaders, Jesus paints a picture of a young man who leaves his home in search of something more in life. This young man begins his journey toward the land of Better-Than-Here with a pocket full of money and a head full of dreams. Soon the young man is broke and without resources to live. Jesus tells the crowd that the young man's misfortune came as a result of wild living. The young man takes a job feeding pigs in a farmer's field.

I can't help visualizing this young man in his misery. I imagine him opening his eyes each morning and thinking about how he ended up in such a bad spot. He trudges to that field day after day, reflecting on times gone by and regretting his choices—every good memory swallowed up by mistake after mistake. While he tosses out the slop to the pigs, he sits alone on the fencepost, talking to himself.

> *Idiot.*
> *How could I be so stupid?*
> *What was I thinking?*
> *Oh, I wish that I could do it all over again...*

There's no reference in the story to how long the young man works in that field. Actually, it's irrelevant to the main point, but I've always been drawn to that part of the story. It reminds me of the times in my life when I've felt alone and trapped in my regret and shame.

How often do you beat yourself up? We all make mistakes, but as women we love to heap criticism on ourselves. If someone says something negative about our size, shape, or style, we're quick to believe what they say. When we look in the mirror and focus on our flaws, we add to the negative parts of our beauty narratives.

I like to say that for every perceived failure, we're adding a stone to our Road of Regret. As that road becomes longer, we convince ourselves that there is something wrong with us. Each time we look back, all we can see are mistakes. Then we come to believe that no matter how hard we try, we'll never be enough. If we stay on the Road of Regret long enough, eventually we will arrive at the entrance to that dark, painful place I call the Land of Shame. Some of you know what I'm talking about.

The Land of Shame has a few streets called Coulda, Shoulda, and Woulda. If you've ever tried and failed at a diet, you may be living with shame. If someone in your life has repeatedly told you that you aren't good enough, you may be living with shame. If your physical appearance is much different than you would like it to be, then you may be living with shame.

Once we end up living in shame, it's hard to break free. Why? Because the sheriff in the Land of Shame is Satan. He likes to keep us in the Land of Shame because he knows that shame holds us back. It makes us too insecure to live fully for God in every area of our lives.

Unfortunately, where there is shame, we will struggle to find beauty.

Satan likes to twist our beauty narratives. Perhaps you've been working out for months, but the weight isn't coming off. One day you get discouraged and eat a pile of cookies. As you bemoan that decision, the Sheriff of Shame (or one of his deputies) won't waste a moment suggesting to you that you're a failure and you should just give up. Or if you're a single woman who would like to have a relationship but are not being asked out by any eligible men, Satan may whisper: "No one is asking you out. You must not be pretty enough." Do you know the motto of the Land of Shame? It's this: "There's no hope. You are stuck here because you can't change."

But there is hope! You can change! The Land of Shame isn't a life sentence, no matter what the Sheriff has whispered into your ear.

My favorite part of the Prodigal Son's story is found in verses 17-19.

Read Luke 15:17-19. How does verse 17 begin?

When...

Once we end up living in shame, it's hard to break free.

What realization does the young man make?

This is the moment of great revelation! It is the moment when he realizes that he doesn't have to live that way any longer.

Though Jesus tells this story to make a point about repentance, it also speaks to us about leaving places where we don't belong. I picture the young man hopping down off that pigpen fence and hustling back to his childhood home. He may not have known what was waiting for him at home, but he didn't waste any time getting away from the place where he knew he didn't belong.

When you think about the "places" in your beauty narrative that burn or tear your heart, those are the places where you may be living in the Land of Shame. Isn't it time to break free and run back home to the Father? If you let Him, He will love you and restore all of the hurting places in your heart and mind.

Have you paved a Road of Regret? What are the parts of your beauty narrative that you associate with regret (for things you should have done but didn't)?

As the sheriff of the Land of Shame, Satan seeks to add to his town population. He already knows what his end looks like, but that doesn't deter him from trying to ruin the lives of as many people as possible. If we are created in the image of God, then Satan wants to undermine our understanding of what being made in the image of God really means and how it should impact our lives. Because the Scriptures tell us that God is love, we can expect that Satan will try to convince us by whatever means necessary that God does not love us.

Read John 8:44. What do we learn from this verse about Satan's character?

How has Satan used lies to begin, continue, or exaggerate your ugly struggle with beauty?

Read John 10:10 in the margin. Here Jesus uses shepherding as an analogy to contrast His purpose with Satan's purpose. How does Jesus describe His purpose?

How does He describe Satan's purpose?

So, knowing that Satan uses lies for the purpose of destroying us, how can we break free from the Land of Shame?

Read John 8:32 in the margin. According to this verse, what sets us free?

Truth is the key that sets us free. Throughout this study we are going to clothe our hearts, minds, and bodies with the power of God's truth. Because God created us, loves us, and sent Jesus to deliver us and bring us a rich and satisfying life, we can trust God's truth to lead us out of the Land of Shame toward everlasting freedom. We can't leave the Land of Shame by our own power; we have to deploy the resource of God's truth in order to break free from the shame caused by our enemy's lies and win our ugly struggle with beauty.

What are some truths from God's Word about who God is and His plan for your life that you need to lean into as you battle to win your ugly struggle with beauty?

Look up 2 Corinthians 10:3-5. According to verse 5, how do we destroy the strongholds that keep us captive?

"The thief's purpose is to steal and kill and destroy. My purpose is to give them a rich and satisfying life." (John 10:10)

"And you will know the truth, and the truth will set you free." (John 8:32)

List below some of the lies we encounter as women when it comes to beauty. How can these lies make us captives in the Land of Shame?

Let's conclude our study today by rewriting the negative and untrue portions of our beauty narratives.

Refer to your beauty narrative on page 22 (or at the back of the book) as you complete the chart below. In the left column, list the portions of your beauty narrative that you know are not true in God's eyes. In the right column, replace that faulty narrative with truth from God's Word. Use a print or online Bible concordance to locate specific Scriptures that convey God's perspective.

Portions of my beauty narrative that are not true:	What God says about me that is the truth:

Live It Out

1. What is one thing that God impressed upon your heart during today's study?

2. Do you have a sense or leading from God about what you need to think or do differently as a result of what you've studied?

Most of us have lived in the Land of Shame at one point or another. If you are there now, you don't have to stay! Tell God that you are ready to break free from the Land of Shame, and ask Him to use the truth that you identified today to break the hold that shame has had on your life.

If you don't feel that you are living in the Land of Shame, then take some time to pray for your sisters in Christ who need to find freedom.

Day 4: Defeating the Enemies of Comparison and Competition

Beauty Mark
You can kill comparison and competition with love!

Beauty Regimen

We spent the past two days studying shame and how it impacts our beauty narratives. I love how Rahab's story reminds us that no matter what we've been called, God has created a new narrative for us—a storyline in which we are treasured and valued for who He has created us to be.

Yet even as we deal with our beauty narratives, we also encounter real-time struggles with processing the images about beauty that we interact with on a daily basis. For me, the grocery store checkout line can be a tricky place to be.

I like to read the covers of magazines while I wait in the checkout line. Yes, I know that those photos are enhanced, but I still find myself looking at them sometimes to see how I compare. (Can you relate?) For years, magazine covers featuring celebrities with two rows of even, shining white teeth would catch my attention, and as I would gaze at the pictures, my thoughts and feelings would vacillate between longing and guilt. In one moment I would think, *If I had beautiful teeth like that, I would never stop smiling and would really feel beautiful.* In the next moment, guilt would set in and I would think, *Seriously? What's wrong with you? Stop thinking about this! There are more important issues in the world than your two front teeth. Get over it!*

Over the years, I've discovered that along with the weapon of shame, the Sheriff of Shame carries two guns: comparison and competition. With comparison, we're always looking at other women to see how we are similar or different in our size, shape, or style. When it comes to competition, we observe other women to see how close or far they are to our personal beauty standards. Now, comparison and competition are silent contests. We don't like to admit them or talk about them, but we live them.

If we're looking at images in magazines or hanging out with our girl-friends, we shouldn't be surprised when we hear whispers or suggestions such as these:

Did she lose weight? Is she skinnier than you?
Look at her new hair style! She's going to get more attention than you the next time that you go out.
Check out the bags under her eyes! You better make sure that you don't get those!
Aren't you glad that you don't have hips that wide?

Comparison and competition fuel our ugly struggle with beauty in three ways:

1. They cause us to always look for what's wrong in us, or what I like to call "flaw finding."
2. They create a barrier between us and other women so that connection is stifled or even suffocated.
3. They create collateral damage in other areas of our lives such as our finances and other relationships.

Today we're going to identify the places where we feel pressure to measure up, and then we're going to look at the story of Rachel and Leah and see the impact that comparison and competition had on their lives. Finally, we'll discover how we can disarm these two destructive "guns" and eliminate them from our ugly struggle with beauty.

As I mentioned in the introduction, I don't have anything against the beauty industry. In fact, I love finding clothes, shoes, and beauty products that make me look great at a great price. Yet I recognize that the constant feed of beauty-related messages can be overwhelming at times. I also must admit that even though I see those airbrushed images of celebrities, my brain doesn't always remember that those images aren't real. If I'm having a bad day, I might compare myself against someone's hair or hips—and it never turns out in my favor.

When you think about all of the messages about beauty as well as your personal struggles with size, shape, or style, how much pressure do you feel to fit in with our culture's definition of beauty?

____ **Extreme pressure**
____ **A lot of pressure**
____ **Some pressure**
____ **No pressure**

There was a time when I would have checked "a lot of pressure." Thankfully, now I can check "some pressure." After working in sales for a few years and dealing with my beauty baggage for many more, I can happily say that I feel less pressure than before. But it has been a process!

The story of Jacob, Rachel, and Leah is in found in Genesis 29:15-33; 30:1-24. The background of the story is that Jacob, the son of Isaac and Rebekah, traveled to stay with an uncle named Laban. While Jacob later would receive an inheritance after his father died, Jacob arrived at his uncle's home without any property or money of his own. So Laban let Jacob work for him. While working for his uncle, Jacob fell in love with Laban's daughter Rachel.

In Genesis 29:17, physical descriptions of Rachel and Leah are given. How is each woman described?

Rachel   **Leah**

Notice how Leah is described with "no sparkle in [her] eyes." Other translations refer to Leah as "tender-eyed," meaning that she had some type of eye defect and therefore was less physically attractive than her sister.[7]

It's not hard to imagine that more attention likely went to Leah's younger sister, Rachel. What are some of the things that Leah might have heard people saying over and over again about her sister but not about her?

In Genesis 29:25, we see that Jacob woke up the morning after his marriage to discover he had married Leah, not Rachel. While the responsibility for such a deceptive act rested wholly with Laban, take a moment and put yourself in Leah's sandals.

What must Leah have felt as Jacob raged about another woman he wanted to be married to instead of her?

So filled with love for Rachel, Jacob immediately agreed to work seven more years for her, and so Laban gave Rachel to Jacob in marriage too. Not only was Leah not Jacob's first choice, she did not have Jacob's love. Adding to her pain, Leah then had to share her husband because of a situation created by her father, but it was her situation nonetheless.

Read Genesis 29:31. How did God respond to Leah?

Describe the competition that ensued between the two women.

As you read Genesis 30:1-8, note how Rachel handled the situation. What kind of heart did Rachel seem to have?

What did Rachel proclaim in verse 8?

There are times when the story of Jacob, Rachel, and Leah seems like an ancient episode of *The Jerry Springer Show* or *The Maury Show*. Jacob was the baby daddy while Rachel and Leah were the baby mamas fighting over who would get his love. Yet as we read their stories, we see that the competition between the women ruined their relationship with each other and strained other relationships in their families.

You may know what it's like to be compared to someone, whether the comparison was or is by height, weight, eye color, or shape. Comparisons divide us and can lead to a competition where there are no winners.

When you see magazine photos of celebrities or actresses, how often do you compare yourself to what you see in the photos?

___ Always
___ Sometimes
___ Never

Here's a story from a friend of mine about what it was like being compared to other girls at an early age:

As early as nine years old and into my early teens, I have vivid memories of standing next to my cousins and being judged by adult female family members. Their commentary was blazed into my memory:

> "Her breasts are bigger than so-and-sos."
> "She has a prettier smile."
> "Her attitude is much better."
> "She's maturing faster. Did she start her period?"

Oddly enough, this scenario seemed normal. In my world, it was normal to worry about what other people thought of me. It was OK to want people to like me. In order to be found acceptable, I wondered about how to make my boobs bigger (even though I was well endowed for my petite frame) or how often I needed to suck in my gut so that I could appear thinner.

Those comparisons created a lot of problems between my cousins and me. We were friends, but once we were pitted against each other everything became a competition.[8]

Were you ever compared physically to another woman, either as a child or an adult? If so, how did you feel about the comparisons?

What feelings and memories still linger today?

If we define competition as a desire to match or one-up another woman in an area of size, shape, or style, are there any places in your life where you are engaged in a silent competition?

What are some ways that you have seen Christian women comparing or competing against one another in church?

How have the relationships between the women been impacted as a result?

Christian women aren't immune to comparison or competition. I grew up in a church where women wore magnificent hats on Sunday. During Easter and Christmas seasons, the hat competition was fierce!

Let's be honest for a moment about how we check out each other when we come to church each week. It's like a silent version of *America's Next Top Model*. When we see women come into church, we're often mentally putting them on display whether we realize it or not. Yes, it's not something we like to admit, but come on ladies, let's keep it real! It may go something like this. First we quickly scan what she's wearing to find out if it's acceptable and then to ascertain whether or not she's dressed better than us. Then we'll do a quick scan of her shoes before leaping back up to check out her hair and jewelry. Have you ever found yourself doing that? Most of us have.

There's a difference between noticing and comparing. As far as I am concerned, the difference comes down to whether or not I'm looking for something to *compliment* or something to *criticize*.

If we want to elevate the conversation one more level, the weapon that overpowers competition and comparison is *love*.

Look up 1 Corinthians 13:4-7 and write it in the space below. These verses show us how love is the antidote to comparison and competition.

How can these verses remind you to look at other women with love, rather than with an attitude of comparison and competition?

If you begin to look at all women with love, how could that help you to look at yourself less critically?

Challenge yourself to stop mentally competing with other women. Choose instead to compliment others, letting them know that you are for them, rather than competing against them. You'll be amazed at the number of women who will be uplifted and encouraged by your words. It's a strategy that will enable to you win too!

Live It Out

1. What is one thing that God impressed upon your heart during today's study?

2. Do you have a sense or leading from God about what you need to think or do differently as a result of what you've studied?

Talk with God

Don't be ashamed to admit that you've struggled with comparing yourself or competing with other women. Confess that struggle before God. Ask for forgiveness and, most of all, for God to fill your heart with love for all women so that you see them as your beautiful sisters in Christ, not your competition.

Day 5: Protecting the Truth

Beauty Mark
You are beautiful because God made you!

Beauty Regimen

Imagine showing up to your house after a week-long vacation and your home's front door is wide open. Pushing past those instant feelings of fear and disbelief, you creep up to the open doorway and peek inside. Another surprise awaits! All of the windows are open too.

If you are anything like me, your first thought would be to hustle back to your car and dial 911. Why? Houses with wide open doors and windows don't feel safe. When we're in our homes, our private space, it's our doors and windows that help us feel protected. Without that protection, unwelcome guests may come into our space with their own agendas.

When it comes to our ugly struggle with beauty, our hearts, minds, and bodies also need protection. We all have vulnerable places that are at risk for damage. Depending on your beauty narrative, you may have already experienced some damage, so care must be taken to prevent additional or future destruction.

A few years ago, I stayed with friends who installed an alarm system in their home. Since there would be times when I'd arrive at the house before the family, they wanted to teach me how to turn the system on and off. As we walked through the house, the husband showed me the different sensors placed above the doorways and on the home's windows. The sensors were placed in those areas because they were the most vulnerable places in a home and the likely point of entry by a burglar.

Of course, the next day I arrived at the house and promptly set off the alarm. My mistake was that I activated a sensor but couldn't unlock the door in time. I jumped as the alarm sounded, creating quite a noise in their cul de sac. Quite embarrassing! Yet if I had been an intruder, that loud alarm would have been quite a convincing deterrent.

When I think about our ugly struggle with beauty and the impact it has on our hearts, it is clear to me that we must have sensors for the sensitive, vulnerable places. Where or when are you most vulnerable or sensitive when it comes to the topic of beauty? Maybe you feel vulnerable when you are out with your girlfriends and everyone has a boyfriend or husband except for you. Or maybe it's when you're with your mom or sister and one of them reminds you that you were much skinnier in high school. In situations like those, you need to establish sensors; and when the sensors go off, you've got to be ready for battle and to fight back!

Today we're going to talk about what it means to establish beauty-sensors and how to fight back when those sensors go off. You'll know that you're fighting back when those vulnerable events happen yet you later find yourself standing strong in God's truth rather than lying wounded in a pool of insecurity while eating a carton of ice cream.

Earlier this week we learned how Satan uses lies to convince us to believe that we could never be beautiful. His goal is to discourage us from living fully and trusting God in every area of our lives.

Protecting our hearts is serious business! Think about protecting your heart like the Secret Service protects the president of the United States. As the most powerful person in the world, the president is our country's leader and an asset to be protected. While we might think that the safest place for the president to be would be a mile underground in a concrete bunker, the role of the Secret Service is to help the president to be as available to others as possible while providing protection. Since there can be a threat to the president's life at any time, Secret Service agents must be ready for anything. As one agent described their approach, "Protection is an art form," meaning that protection has to adjust and adapt depending on the circumstances.[9] They must continually adjust, determining what to keep out as well as what to allow in. The same is true when it comes to guarding our hearts.

Strong's Concordance defines our heart as our inner self, so what we are to guard is actually a combination of our heart and mind, representing our emotions and our thoughts, respectively.[10]

Read Proverbs 4:23 in the margin. Why is it imperative that we guard our hearts?

Guard your heart
above all else,
    for it determines
        the course of
        your life.
(Proverbs 4:23)

Focus on the word *guard*. Give some examples of other things in life that we guard:

To help you know what situations you need to guard against related to beauty, think about and write a brief answer to the following questions:

When do I tend to feel the most insecure as it pertains to my body size, shape, or style?

What are some of the websites or magazines that can make me feel bad about myself after I read them?

Who are the friends/family members/acquaintances who tend to make critical comments about my appearance?

When I experience beauty-related pain, how does it change the way I view myself?

If you didn't connect with the Secret Service analogy, here's another. Think about your heart like a garden. Picture your garden. Visually populate it with flowers or vegetables—your preference. Now, picture a long afternoon of rain followed by a few days of hot sun. While your garden is growing, there are some intruders who will try to pop up as well: weeds.

What's the problem with weeds? Well, weeds siphon the nourishment from the plants that will actually produce something of value. Weeds don't produce anything of value; they only produce more weeds. Furthermore, weeds grow quickly, so any prolonged period of inattention can spell disaster. If you've been gardening for any length of time, you know that when you see a weed, you pluck it out as soon as possible.

In our world, the Internet gives everyone a platform and a voice to share his or her opinion. It also provides endless opportunities for businesses to infiltrate their sales messages into almost every aspect of our lives. This means that there are a lot of "weeds" in the form of beauty-related messages that will never encourage or uplift your heart but, instead, will overrun your heart with feelings of inadequacy and struggle, leading to discouragement.

Think about "weeds" such as the constantly recurring thoughts that you might have about your physical flaws. What are some of those recurring thoughts?

Look up Colossians 2:8 and write it the margin. Circle the word *captive* (some translations may use *capture*, *enslave*, or *cheat*).

In this verse, the word *captive* is defined as to "make victim by fraud."[11] What are some of the ways that you see women, including yourself, being taken captive by the world's concept of beauty?

The Apostle Paul refers to two influences that we can be taken captive through, becoming victims by fraud. What are these influences?

Why are God's weapons more effective than our efforts?

Extra Insight:

Did you ever notice that the armor of God does not include pants? I didn't until someone pointed it out to me. Forgive me, but I had a good laugh over that one!

We never have to feel helpless in our ugly struggle with beauty! Ephesians 6:10-17 outlines the weapons that God gives us to fight. Ladies, we may be talking about beauty, but our battle—our ugly struggle with beauty—is against the enemy of our souls!

Look up Ephesians 6:10-17 and list the weapons God gives us that we can use to win our ugly struggle with beauty:

Which weapons do you need to deploy *right now* in your ugly struggle with beauty?

As we conclude our study today, let's create a framework for how we can set up our security system and attack plan. Follow the prompts below to customize your own plan. There are verses in parentheses that you can read through as part of this exercise.

Follow the prompts below to complete your plan.

1. Identify the risk (area of vulnerability). (Psalm 139)

When it comes to my ugly struggle with beauty, I am most vulnerable when _____
_____.

2. Notice when the alarm sounds. (Proverbs 14:16)

My struggle begins when _____
_____.

3. Call on God and trust friends for help. (James 4:7-8; Hebrews 4:16; Ecclesiastes 4:9-11)

When my struggle begins, I need to take a deep breath and focus on God and His truth. These are the things I need to remember:

4. Overpower the threat. (1 Corinthians 10:13; 2 Corinthians 10:5)

Here are some Bible verses I need to write down and/or memorize in order to fight back and overcome my beauty-related insecurities:

5. Declare victory! (John 16:33)

I know that I am victorious when the following happens:

___ My heart doesn't sink into pain and despair after hurtful comments or experiences.
___ My mind doesn't drift off into harmful, destructive shame statements.
___ My heart and mind are focused on God's truth.
___ I don't attack the person or people involved in the situation.
___ Other:

Live It Out

1. What is one thing that God impressed upon your heart during today's study?

2. Do you have a sense or leading from God about what you need to think or do differently as a result of what you've studied?

Talk with God

Now that you've got a framework for how to guard your heart, ask God to help you activate it. If you haven't been able to come up with Scripture verses you need to memorize as part of your plan, ask God to lead you to those verses that *you* need in order to win your ugly struggle with beauty.

ALL ABOARD THE STRUGGLE BUS

Beauty is a description of three things:

1. Our _____.

2 Our _____.

3. Our _____.

We have an _____ _____ with beauty that we don't want to fight.

Now the man and his wife were both naked, but they felt no _____.
(Genesis 2:25)

At that moment their eyes were opened, and they suddenly felt shame at their nakedness. So they sewed fig leaves together to cover themselves. When the cool evening breezes were blowing, the man and his wife heard the LORD God walking about in the garden. So they hid from the LORD God among the trees. (Genesis 3:7-8)

Shame is this feeling deep inside that there is something _____ with us.

Shame tells a story that we are _____ _____.

A lie that is believed as the truth will affect us as if it was _____.

The stories that we tell ourselves about our beauty—I call those stories our

_____ _____.

When we don't believe that we are _____ we are going to look to other

people and other things to convince us that we are _____.

Guard your heart above all else,
for it determines the course of your life.
(Proverbs 4:23)

We need _____ to believe that we are enough in a world that is constantly showing us our faults and our failures.

Week 2

DEFINING DIVINE BEAUTY

Memory Verse

But now you must be holy in everything you do, just as God who chose you is holy. For the Scriptures say, "You must be holy because I am holy."

(1 Peter 1:15-16)

This Week's Theme
When we know who God is, then we will understand beauty.

Does God really care about beauty?

That's the question that many well-meaning, Jesus-loving Christian women want to know. If we take our cues from what we see in culture, we might believe that the topic of beauty is shallow or insignificant. But that's not how God sees beauty. Like everything else God created, beauty has a purpose.

Although we may struggle with our "relationship" with beauty, our God shows us the importance of physical beauty. The evidence of this beauty is all around for us to see and enjoy. Most of all, beauty is a tangible reminder for us to worship God for who He is and all that He does for us.

This week we're going to tackle the definition of beauty, starting with who God is. When we know who God is, that gives us a definition of beauty that not only helps us to overcome our ugly struggle but also serves as a compass, pointing us to God and equipping us to point others to God as well. When we're moving toward God, we avoid the Road of Regret or an unintentional stay in the Land of Shame. We'll discuss how we can remain connected to God's beauty when we pursue and walk in holiness. Finally, we'll pivot and look at how God reveals beauty in the world around us.

Day 1: God Defines Beauty

Beauty Mark

Divine beauty is the true, good, and beautiful nature of God.

Beauty Regimen

A few times a year, I pilgrimage an hour north of my home to IKEA with a few girlfriends. Even though an hour's drive isn't very far, it's far enough for the trip to be special each time we go. Our purpose for going to IKEA is simple. We want to "ooh" and "aah" and find lots of pretty things.

IKEA houses three floors of beautiful items that elicit thousands of "ooh" and "aah" moments. The girls and I love mentally redecorating the different rooms of our homes as we weave in and out of different displays and vignettes. As we walk and talk, we judge the merchandise according to what we find pleasing or displeasing to look at.

One of us might point to a set of bookcases, curtains, or patterned textile and exclaim, "Oh, don't you just love how this looks!" Sometime we'll agree with her. Sometimes we won't. We don't have any rules regarding what we love and what we don't; it's a matter of personal preference.

Doesn't it seem that defining beauty is often a matter of personal preference? Defining beauty is a difficult task. Philosophers argue whether beauty is objective or subjective.[1] Does it matter that we all have a different application of the definition? Can something be beautiful if one person says it is and another person says it isn't? If that is the case, then where does that leave us? Does our beauty rely on the opinions and perceptions of others or on our own ideas?

In our culture, there is no absolute definition of beauty. Scientists have tried to apply objective constructs to measure beauty. They've measured for proportionality and symmetry or harmony, but to no avail. Our best human thinking about beauty is caught up in a black hole that just absorbs our inputs and opinions but never reveals a true answer. This is why I believe that the phrase "Beauty is in the eye of the beholder" is the most dangerous phrase a woman could ever believe. These words are supposed to bring some sort of freedom to proclaim beauty in anyone or anything. Unfortunately, it also suggests that beauty can be created or destroyed by anyone and everyone who weighs in with an opinion. My friends, we are caught in a horrible, swirling vortex of opinion about beauty without a clear direction. In the whirlwind, opinions from media, advertisers, family, and friends strike at our hearts and minds with no protection or filter. Too many of us are suffering as a result.

"Make me beautiful." This was the simple request that freelance journalist Esther Honig sent to nearly fifty freelance designers from dozens of countries around the world, along with an unaltered image of herself. Those freelancers applied their individual aesthetic and sent Esther their altered images of herself. She admits that some of the images were shocking at first. In some of the photos, Esther's appearance doesn't change much; there is just some airbrushing of her skin. Other freelance artists changed her eye color, skin tone, hair color, or even hair style. Interestingly enough, there were a few incidences of artists from the same country who returned radically different images.

Media outlet Buzzfeed published the photos in June 2014.[2] In an interview, this is how Esther summed up the experience: "What I've learned from the project is this: Photoshop [may] allow us to achieve our unobtainable standards of beauty, but when we compare those standards on a global scale, achieving the ideal remains all the more illusive."[3]

You can find a video presentation of Esther's project, "Before & After," on her website.[4] She has appeared on multiple television shows and has shared her experience in many social media articles. Since making her project public, a few other women of different races and body sizes have duplicated her challenge, sending photos of themselves to designers with the request to be made beautiful.

Even if we'd never admit it, we *all* are seekers of beauty. We want to know what real beauty is because we desire beauty in the deepest level of our being, and the thought of not being beautiful inflicts a terrible pain.

As I mentioned earlier in our study, a couple of years ago I conducted a survey about beauty among a group of more than five hundred women called *Created with Curves*. One of the questions I asked was "How do you define beauty?" Here are some of the responses:

> "You must have a beautiful heart to have complete beauty."
> "Being comfortable in your own skin."
> "Beauty is when you feel good about how you look."
> "What is on the inside, not on the outside."
> "Friendly, loving, nice, kind, gracious, and hospitable."
> "Not me."

As might be expected, many of the definitions included words such as *loving, kind*, and *confident*. Some of the physical characteristics included words such as *healthy, fit*, and *proportionate features*. I appreciated one participant who added that cleanliness should be part of the definition of beauty. Amen, sister.

How do *you* define beauty?

Why do we have so many different definitions of beauty? Should we allow beauty to be defined any way that we want to define it? I believe that if we understand who God is, then we will understand beauty.

As Christians, when we speak of the meaning and origin of beauty, the nature of God should anchor our discussion. Any attempt to explain beauty must stem from God's divine character—and nothing else—because God is the originator of beauty. Theologian R. C. Sproul says that God is the "Author of all beauty" because God is the source and He sets the standard for beauty.[5] This is why we call the highest form of beauty *divine beauty*.

While God cannot be explained or defined in human terms, He shows us His character and nature in the Scriptures. Why? God wants us to know Him. We need to know God because He is our Creator. We also need to know God if we want to truly know ourselves. Through the Scriptures we discover many qualities of God's character, but I'd like to highlight three that are integrally related to God's divine beauty:

1. God is TRUTH.
2. God is GOOD.
3. God is BEAUTIFUL.[6]

Your spiritual journey or worldview will determine how these three statements about God resonate with you. Many people struggle to accept absolutes. It's considered polite in our culture to adopt an "anything goes" mentality about life. Sometimes we hesitate to apply a right-or-wrong value to any standard because we fear labels such as intolerant, prejudiced, or ignorant. Yet God is absolute. He is not relative to anything in our world. Even if your view of God is filled with questions, chances are you would agree that God—the Creator of the universe—has no equal. This means that whatever quality we ascribe to God, God is the ultimate of that quality. No one and nothing is a better example or version of that quality.

So let's see what the Bible has to say about these three qualities of God.

1. God is TRUTH.

We live in a world that encourages people to "follow their heart" or "do what feels right." When it comes to our culture's perspective on beauty, it's best summed up by "anything and everything goes!" While that kind of permissive mind-set seems freeing, that carefree viewpoint actually creates confusion.

Through the Scriptures and God's revelation of Himself in Christ, God shows us absolute truth—complete and invariable truth or realities. We're going to look at what the Bible says about God's character and why we can trust in God's truth.

Look up Numbers 23:19 and Hebrews 6:18. What do both verses say about God?

If it is impossible for God to lie, then what God says about us in the Bible is true. Yet there are times when we doubt God's words as they apply to us.

Are there any areas where you struggle to accept God's truth as the absolute, final authority in your life?

Read Colossians 2:3 in the margin. This verse points to the fact that God holds a monopoly on two other qualities related to truth. What are these two qualities?

Trusting in God's truth is precious to us, friends! In a world that wants us to chase beauty down endless dead-end streets, we can find God's truth about who He is and what He says in Scripture. When we trust in God's truth, we don't have to ask the question "Am I beautiful?" anymore. God's answer is always yes.

2. God is GOOD.

I grew up in a church where people said, "God is good all the time and all the time, God is good." This particular cliché has appeared in sermons and songs for many years. It has been a common greeting used by individuals in good times as well as difficult times.

In Matthew 19:17, Jesus declares, "There is only One who is good." Because God is always good, He is always for our good, even in those times we don't understand. If you struggle with a physical or mental condition or a life circumstance that just doesn't seem fair, you may have wondered whether or not God is truly good. If we're honest, sometimes in the midst of our struggles we think that if God were good, then He wouldn't let us suffer.

Yet God's goodness isn't tied to our circumstances. God is good because His character is perfect goodness. There is no evil found anywhere in God's character.

The Book of Psalms records numerous accolades of praise for God's goodness, no matter the circumstances or seasons of life.

In him lie hidden all the treasures of wisdom and knowledge. (Colossians 2:3)

Extra Insight:

"Because God is absolute truth, I will believe what He says and live accordingly." —Bill Bright[7]

This is the message
we heard from
Jesus and now
declare to you: God
is light, and there
is no darkness
in him at all.
(1 John 1:5)

Extra Insight:

"The highest good,
than which there is
no higher, is God,
and consequently
He is unchangeable
good, hence truly
eternal and truly
immortal. All other
good things are
only from Him."
—Augustine
of Hippo[8]

"God is summum
bonum, the
chiefest good."
—Arthur W. Pink[9]

According to the following psalms, what are some of the characteristics of God's goodness? How does God's goodness benefit us?

Psalm 100:5

Psalm 107:8

Psalm 119:65-68

Read 1 John 1:5 in the margin. How does this verse characterize God's goodness in a different way?

Do you believe that God is good all the time and all the time, God is good? I've realized in my own life that embracing God's goodness comes as the result of experiencing God's goodness. There will always be situations in life that we don't understand, but there is a God who does understand. Not only that, but He has the power to redeem the pain and heartache that we've experienced. God can bring good out of any circumstance!

3. God is BEAUTIFUL.

While it might feel a bit odd to define "divine beauty" by redundantly using the word *beautiful*, frankly there is no better word to use when describing God. The opposite of *beauty* is *ugliness*, which implies distastefulness. Since we've just studied God's goodness, we know that there is nothing ugly about God.

I love how pastor and author John Piper describes God's beauty as a reflection of His glory.[10] God's glory is hard to wrap our minds around, but it is the combination of all that God is. Of course, we can't understand *all* that God is, but we can understand a little bit. When we fathom each aspect of God's character and magnify it to the level of our comprehension, then we may have an inkling of God's glory. Piper identifies the relationship between God's glory and God's beauty: "If we admire the glory of God, we are admiring God's beauty. If the glory of God has an effect in our lives, God's beauty is having an effect. If God acts to magnify this glory, he is acting to magnify his beauty."[11]

So the perfection of God's character is His glory, and every time God's glory is on display, the beauty of God shines through.

Read Psalm 27:4 in the margin. What request does the psalmist make of God?

One thing I ask from the LORD,
     this only do
       I seek:
that I may dwell
in the house of
the LORD
     all the days
     of my life,
to gaze on the
beauty of the LORD
     and to seek him
     in his temple.
(Psalm 27:4 NIV)

Based on our conversation about glory and beauty, why would the psalmist desire such an experience?

Now that we've looked at what the Bible says about God's truth, goodness, and beauty, let us summarize His character in these three areas:

1. Since God is TRUTH, God cannot lie or undermine Himself. Therefore, what He declares as truth is absolute and cannot be undermined or discredited as not true—including what He says about us.
2. Since God is GOOD, He is void of anything that is not good, and everything that is good has its origins in God.
3. Since God is BEAUTIFUL, He has no ugliness or distortion, and His beauty transcends our hearts and minds and soaks into our souls.

This picture of God is the picture of divine beauty.

Divine beauty: the true, good, and beautiful nature of God.

How does this definition of divine beauty compare or contrast with some of the more popular cultural definitions of beauty?

Divine beauty is the highest form of beauty possible. In our humanity, it's impossible for us to attain the same level of beauty as God, but we *can* reflect His character—His divine beauty—in our lives.

Which of these three aspects or characteristics of God's divine beauty do you need to reflect more often?

When we know God's character, then we know more about who we are. The blessing for us is that God is the ultimate of all that we desire.

When we deepen our understanding and our relationship with the true, good, and beautiful God, we become more like Him in every way. And that's a beautiful thing!

Live It Out

1. What is one thing that God impressed upon your heart during today's study?

2. Do you have a sense or leading from God about what you need to think or do differently as a result of what you've studied?

Talk with God

Knowing God for who He really is changes you! When you *know God's truth*, you are able to think differently. When you *recognize God's goodness*, you are able to see things differently. Finally, when you *embrace God's beauty*, you are able to see yourself differently, recognizing God's beauty within you. For today, reflect on God's character and how you need to know God more. The best way to know God is to discover Him though Bible study, life experience, and most of all, prayer.

Day 2: The Beauty of Holiness

Beauty Mark
Living in holiness is the key to experiencing God's blessing of beauty.

Beauty Regimen

There's a word that describes the special uniqueness of God: *holy*. The ancient meaning of *holy* is "set apart."[12] God is holy or set apart because His nature is the ultimate and unmatched in truth, goodness, and beauty. His nature provides a different measuring stick than our culture's standards for truth, goodness, and beauty.

Unfortunately, using the words *holy* and *holiness* in our culture tends to spark accusations of intolerance, prejudice, or extremism. This is regrettable, because being holy should be a desirable distinction. The essence of being holy is being set apart as different than the world—seeking to be separate from sin and devoted to God. To become holy is to become more like God.

So could it be that when we establish an eternal connection with God and we embrace our standing as children being created in His image and set apart for His service, then we realize that we are beautiful—not because of anything we've done but simply because we are made in the image of a holy and beautiful God?

The classic movie *Mean Girls* provides a picture of how our culture can manipulate the idea of being set apart. Though no one would argue that the Plastics clique was holy, queen bee Regina and crew made it clear that they were a cut above the rest of the school. The Plastics used their beauty to create a divide between them and others in order to dominate and intimidate.

Being made in the image of God doesn't make us gods. Repeat: *being created in the image of God does not make us gods.* There is only one God, and we are not Him. Rather, being created in God's image means that we should never believe anything that is said about us that is inconsistent with God's character. When we look in the mirror, we should remember that we are created in God's image. Furthermore, God invites us to connect with Him and share in His holy nature by walking in His truth, goodness, and beauty.

Because our culture continues to drift farther and farther away from God, it should be getting easier to identify Christians, right? There should be a huge difference between the attitudes, beliefs, and behaviors of Christians and non-Christians—including how we manage the topic of beauty. Well, I don't know about you, but I'm not seeing too much of a difference. Bummer.

The Apostle Peter wrote to believers in Asia and other countries, encouraging them to pursue Christ even as they endured the inevitable trials that accompanied the Christian life. He reminded them that their faith would grow during those trials and called them to holiness—to champion a different standard of living than those around them.

Read 1 Peter 1:14-16. What is the word in verse 14 that summarizes the difference in behavior between the old way of living and the new way of living in Christ? (The first letter is given.)

O _____

"The essence of God is holiness. Holiness is a divine attribute. God is pure. There is no sin, evil or darkness in God....God cannot not be holy in the same way that God cannot not be love."
—James Bryan Smith[13]

Now read 1 Corinthians 6:19-20 in the margin. Where is the temple of the Holy Spirit?

According to this verse, why does God have the right to command us to live in holiness? What does it mean that we were bought with a price?

How are we to respond?

I don't know about you, but it seems strange that I can read 1 Corinthians 6:19-20 and still have an ugly struggle with beauty. Let's reflect for a moment: Almighty God chooses to let His Spirit inhabit our human bodies. Seriously? And we're complaining about our cellulite and the size of our hips!

Actually, our struggle with beauty has to do with holiness. To unpack this, let's look to the story of the Israelites. When they were released from captivity in Egypt, they were on their own for the first time in more than four hundred years. No longer were the Egyptians telling them what to do and how to live. As Moses led them out of slavery, they needed a new rule of law and order to give them structure and direction. After giving them the Ten Commandments, God outlined a new template for living—specifics for every area of life, including blessings and punishments, which we find in the Book of Leviticus. While it may seem to us that God repeated Himself over and over again, God was impressing upon the Israelites that they no longer needed to follow the crowd and take their cues from the people groups living around them. In fact, it would be to their detriment to do so because God's blessing would not be with them if they wandered astray.

We do not live under the Law anymore, but we can look back and see that although our relationship with God is different, God Himself has not changed.

Read the following verses, comparing those from the Old Testament to those in the New Testament. What is the running theme throughout?

Old Testament	New Testament
Leviticus 11:44-45	1 Peter 2:9
Leviticus 20:7-8	1 Thessalonians 4:7
Leviticus 20:26	2 Timothy 1:9

Running Theme:

In every verse, God calls His people to turn away from the standard of living that opposes His sovereignty and to embrace His standard: holiness. However, embracing God's standard goes against our natural inclination. This is why God must *command* us to be holy, rather than merely suggest it. In the New Living Translation, Leviticus 20:26 reads, "You must be holy." This is clearly a command, and we are called to be obedient to it. Yet obedience is an act of submission, a desire of the will. We must *want* to be obedient to God.

So what does our struggle with beauty have to do with holiness and obedience? I believe that most of us deeply desire to be holy and to honor God with how we "live out" beauty in our lives, but there are some areas where we struggle. If we are really being honest, there are some areas where we reject God's way in favor of our own thinking or behavior, which God calls sin. There are other areas where we are uncertain and need guidance. Some of us wonder if there is a list of do's and don'ts for Christian women when it comes to beauty. Sometimes women will ask me in private if God approves of Botox or cosmetic surgery. Other women want to know how much is too much to spend on a piece of clothing or how many pairs of shoes a "good Christian woman" should own.

The truth is that there is no such list because we have freedom in Christ, and we must live by the Spirit. Yet the Apostle Paul wrote to the Christians in Corinth and cautioned them against taking a careless attitude with their freedom in Christ.

Read 1 Corinthians 10:23 in the margin. What is the attitude of the Corinthians and the response that Paul gives them?

I'm pretty sure that when I mentioned Botox and plastic surgery, a few of my Christian sisters' eyes opened wide. *Oh, we aren't sure about those, Barb.* I know, so we're going to talk about them now. Why? Talking about these topics has been off-limits among many "polite" Christian women. We might have hush-hush conversations after Sister Susie comes back after her

You say, "I am allowed to do anything"—but not everything is good for you. You say, "I am allowed to do anything"—but not everything is beneficial. (1 Corinthians 10:23)

Extra Insight:

"The absolute holiness of God should be of great comfort and assurance to us. If God is perfectly holy, then we can be confident that His actions toward us are always perfect and just."
—Jerry Bridges[14]

long "vacation," but these are conversations that we've tended to deem too unspiritual to talk about in Bible study. Again, if God created our bodies, then these topics have spiritual application.

Is getting Botox or having plastic surgery a sin? No, but considering the way that we whisper about some things like plastic surgery, it's no wonder that women are wondering if it is actually a sin. Our reluctance to talk about these and other beauty-related topics as spiritual issues means we often find ourselves struggling to figure out these things on our own without the benefit of godly wisdom and counsel.

What are your thoughts about cosmetic procedures and plastic surgery?

Why do you think some Christian women feel uncomfortable talking about these topics?

What other beauty-related topics do you see causing confusion among Christian women?

Before you think that I've gone wild and am advocating for every woman to run out and get pinched, tucked, plucked, and dyed, take a moment and consider some guidance from the Apostle Paul that applies to any decision we might make in any area of life, including beauty.

Read 1 Corinthians 10:31 in the margin. What counsel do we receive from this verse?

How could you apply this counsel to your clothing closet, beauty regimen, and shopping habits? List a few ideas below.

The implications of this verse reach beyond your own personal decisions. What is the attitude and purpose that must govern *all* of our beauty-related decisions?

Imagine that one of your Christian sisters is considering a tattoo or cosmetic facelift and has come to you for some advice. What questions would you ask her in hopes of allowing her to discover whether or not her desire is consistent with 1 Corinthians 10:31?

It's my hope and desire that each of us will make a commitment to striving for holiness and doing everything for the glory of God. In a world that promises beauty but delivers bad advice and heartache, we can be shining examples of God's divine beauty *if* we live in obedience to Him.

Now, let's go back to the Old Testament one more time before concluding today's study. There's a wonderful framework that we can adopt when thinking through what it takes for us to live in holiness, set apart for God's purposes.

After the Israelites wandered in the desert for forty years, Moses died and Joshua prepared to lead the people across the Jordan River into the Promised Land. God knew that once they settled in the Promised Land, they would once again live among people whose hearts were far from God. So God gave Joshua a template for how to live a life set apart in holiness. This same template can help us to win our ugly struggle with beauty.

Read Joshua 1:8–9 and fill in the blanks. (The wording is based on the New Living Translation.)

1. _____ this Book of Instruction continually.

2. _____ on it day and night…

3. Be sure to _____ everything written in it.

4. Only then will you _____ and succeed in all you do.

Circle the first step to pursuing holiness.

Underline the result of applying these principles.

"This is my command—
be strong and
courageous!
Do not be afraid
or discouraged.
For the LORD your
God is with you
wherever you go."
(Joshua 1:9)

What does verse 8 imply will happen if we omit any of these principles?

Which one do you need to work on most?

Look at the beginning of Joshua 1:9 in the margin. I love that God was commanding Joshua to be strong and courageous. God knew that Joshua would face opponents and obstacles as the Israelites settled into the Promised Land and made it their new home. Yet God didn't tell Joshua to be strong and courageous because Joshua was a good soldier or an emerging leader. God's command to be strong and courageous was based on the fact that God would be by Joshua's side in battle.

Friend, God is by your side in your ugly struggle with beauty. You are not fighting this battle alone. You are not on your own in the battle to overcome the pain of the past. You are not without help in the battle against all Satan wants to do in order to discourage or defeat you. You can be strong in the face of opposition and have courage in the presence of fear because God is with you wherever you go!

Live It Out

1. **What is one thing that God impressed upon your heart during today's study?**

2. **Do you have a sense or leading from God about what you need to think or do differently as a result of what you've studied?**

Talk with God

Review your Live It Out responses and pray about the places where you need to move toward God in obedience. Also, where is God calling you to be strong and courageous in your life? If you've got a leading from God, then pray about that and make a commitment to pursue where God leads.

Day 3: Beauty All Around!

Beauty Mark

God is the creator of beauty, not us.

Beauty Regimen

Can we agree that God created a beautiful world?

If God didn't care about physical beauty, then why did He create sunrises and sunsets that take our breath away? Why did He create fluffy white clouds and blue skies that urge us to finish our work quickly so we can ride our bikes, take a walk, or read on our decks?

If physical beauty is irrelevant or superfluous, then why do we plant flowers and give them to others for important occasions? Every lawn and garden center, florist, and greenhouse is in business because God decided to share His beauty with our world.

Based on what we see around us, God cares about beauty. God could have created the heavens and the earth in a monotone color scheme or black and white, but He didn't. God didn't have to create flowers in breathtaking, vibrant colors, but He did. Our world could have been so different, yet God has revealed His beautiful character in the world around us.

There are so many evidences of God's beauty all around us. Just consider this list of top natural wonders of the world:

Grand Canyon
Aurora Borealis
Paracutin
Harbor of Rio de Janeiro
Mount Everest
Victoria Falls
Great Barrier Reef [15]

I've only been to one of these wonders, and it took thirty hours to get there! A number of years ago, my husband and I visited Victoria Falls, Zimbabwe. During our nine-day trip, I encountered such wonder and beauty that I'll never forget.

There was a God-moment that summed up the trip for me. It was the last day, and we were finally preparing to tour the actual Victoria Falls. As we left our safari vehicles and walked toward the entrance of the falls, we were greeted by hundreds of small monkeys that lived in the area. They playfully ran and bounced along the ground, unafraid of the human visitors. As we moved past our bouncy welcoming committee, we could see a great mist coming up and away from the waterfall.

As we walked to the bottom of the waterfall, the top of a rainbow came into view. Soon the full rainbow appeared, and my eyes filled with tears before I fully realized the reason why. My body sensed God's beauty before my mind could. Then I had this thought: *I'm standing in a place that has had an unending display of God's promise.*

Friends, there are a lot of problems in our world. The ugliness of sin, war, and decay has left an impact on our world, yet God's stamp of beauty on our planet still shines through.

Read Psalm 19:1-4. What are the heavens proclaiming, and to whom?

When we remember that the skies stretch from the east to the west, this means that wherever we look, we see the evidence of God's glory. Think of all the beauty in the skies: clouds, birds, sun, moon, stars, other planets, and galaxies. There are different kinds of clouds, all types of birds, and many different varieties of suns, moons, stars, and planets in our universe—all created by an amazing God.

It's so easy for us to quickly read Genesis 1 without realizing the depth and breadth of all the beauty that God created.

Read the first chapter of Genesis and make a list below of everything it says that God created.

Not only did God create our world but He also put His stamp of approval on it. Scan Genesis 1 again. What phrase is repeated multiple times in this chapter? Write the phrase below and record the numbers of the verses in which it appears:

Check out the Hebrew translation of the word *towb* in the margin. What does it mean?

One of the things that stands out to me when I read Genesis 1 is that God paid special attention to each area of creation. Have you ever thought about that? Next time that you're outside, look at the leaves on the trees. Seriously, God could have created one type of tree, one kind of flower, and so forth. But He didn't. God created all types of sizes, shapes, and colors for our benefit and enjoyment as well as for us to gain insight into who He is.

Read Genesis 1:31. This is the final verse in the chapter that summarizes how God felt about His workmanship up to that point. What subtle change do you notice in the repeated phrase here?

Read Psalm 8:3-4. What is the question David asked? What was he trying to reconcile?

How does Genesis 1:27 gives us one of many answers to that question? Why does God place such value on human beings?

In my opinion, one of the most beautiful places in the world is located thirty minutes outside of La Ceiba, Honduras, at a beautiful resort called the Palma Real Hotel. On several occasions I've had the privilege of visiting this glorious resort nestled between the majestic Cordillera Nombre de Dios mountain range and the foamy blue waters of the Caribbean. Whenever I've visited there, I have staked out a spot where the ocean water crashes against the sandy shore. I love sitting at the water's edge and feeling the remnants of each wave stroke over my toes. Each time I've sat there, scanning the distant coastline of the Caribbean and gazing out onto the water, I've felt an overwhelming sense of God's majesty and power. In those moments it has been just me and God, and I've sensed creation whispering to me, "If God can do this *and* make it look amazing, He can take care of you."

I am convinced that God values physical beauty and intentionally shares it with us.

In your opinion, where is the most beautiful place in the world? How does it look, feel, sound, and smell?

When you are in that place, does it increase your awareness of God or give you a deep sense of God's power? If so, describe how.

Beauty in nature reveals to us the character of God. As we mentioned at the beginning of this week's study, we cannot know beauty until we know God.

Complete this statement: When I look at the world around me, I know that God values beauty because…

Live It Out

1. What is one thing that God impressed upon your heart during today's study?

2. Do you have a sense or leading from God about what you need to think or do differently as a result of what you've studied?

Talk with God

If you get the chance, go outside today and look around you. What do you see? Give thanks today for the beauty of the world around you.

Day 4: Big and Small Beauty

Beauty Mark
God loves and values us.

Beauty Regimen

I am a horticultural grim reaper. My mother-in-law insists that there's hope for me, but there's a pitiful looking rhododendron in my backyard that says "not a chance." This is sad considering that I just love flowers. Yet every spring I stroll through my historic neighborhood, inhaling the deep perfume smell of lilacs, lavender, hydrangeas, and more. Their colors and fragrances speak to a place deep within my soul.

Have you ever thought of why only women are named after flowers? Guys generally aren't named after flowers. The closest name I can think of would be "Bud." Floral-themed names such as Rose, Lily, Magnolia, or Amethyst are generally reserved for women. Is there a relationship between flowers and women? If so, could this relationship provide some insight into how God sees each of us as women? (By the way, my grandmother's name was Magnolia. She was one of the most magnificent people I've ever known. I'll tell you more about her later.)

When I look at flowers, especially the multitude of varieties, I smile. Their array of colors and designs seems endless, and their fragrances are the basis for many of the finest perfumes we wear today. All of this points to the idea that God is intentional about beauty.

Lately I've been watching the leaves on the tall, sturdy trees in my neighborhood turn from dark green to deep red, bright orange, and lemonade yellow. As much as I love the rich green color of summer, I just love it when those fall colors begin streaking their beautiful hues. Who tells them to do that each year?

Matthew 6 is one of my favorite chapters in the Bible. Jesus was teaching a lot of do's and don'ts about life to the crowd. Then he told the crowd not to worry and used God's creation as an example.

Read Matthew 6:25-33. What observations did Jesus make about flowers?

Jesus was teaching the crowd on a hillside. Imagine for a moment what it might have been like standing or sitting outside as Jesus used creation to communicate important truths about God. The crowd experienced an object lesson as they listened to Jesus teach. It's likely they were listening to Jesus' voice as their eyes swept across the hillside, watching the fields of flowers lightly swaying in the breeze.

In verse 29, we see that Jesus said God dressed the flowers more beautifully than King Solomon, the wisest, richest, and perhaps best-dressed man who ever lived. Yet what did Jesus say in verse 30?

Have you ever held a fine, white lily in your hand? Those flowers are fragile and don't last for more than a few weeks, yet God used His exquisite creative eye to design something so beautiful simply for us to enjoy. In this passage, Jesus reminds us that just as God has given such care and attention to the created world around us, God cares for us even more. While flowers may be temporary, their beauty has value—yet we have substantially more value in God's eyes.

Notice that Jesus used the word *clothe* to describe the petals on the flowers. I love this imagery. It speaks to me as a woman, and I love the visual of God dressing the flowers in beauty. God recognizes that we have need for clothing and must cover our bodies, yet God doesn't want us to get caught up in obsessing over what we're going to wear. This obsession relates to those who continuously purchase volumes of clothes as well as those of us who stand in our closets each morning and bemoan the task of getting dressed.

Describe a time when you found yourself obsessing about your next clothing purchase or what you were going to wear.

How often are you uncomfortable in your clothes or self-conscious about what you are wearing?

How can we take proper care and attention with our clothes without being obsessive about it? Where should we draw the line?

When I think about Jesus' words in Matthew 6:28-30 about how God has created and cares for such gorgeous flowers, reminding us of how much God values beauty, I smile. God didn't have to create beautiful flowers. But He wanted to.

Many years ago I homeschooled my three daughters for a brief period of time. It was a wonderful opportunity brought about by some unique circumstances. During that season, I taught the girls how to make jewelry. But in order to teach them, I first had to learn how to do it.

When I first started making jewelry, I stuck with the basic construct: a piece of jewelry wire, clasp, ring, and simple beads. As a novice, I just wanted to make a bracelet that didn't break when I wore it.

As time went on, my knowledge and skill grew. I began to make more than just bracelets, and each piece of jewelry I created looked more and more like the pictures of the jewelry I saw in the magazines. Years later, jewelry making is still a hobby. I can make personalized gifts or even a custom piece if time allows.

One of the things I think about when it comes to jewelry is that the difference between a simple piece of jewelry and a fancy one involves time, skill, value, and materials. While a lovely solid gold bracelet will find a buyer, a bracelet with embellishments and precious stones will gather admirers and competitive buyers along the way. Beauty attracts and commands attention.

God wants us to pay attention to beauty and to recognize His power over all things, both great and small. God pays attention to the big details of the universe as well as the fine details of each individual flower in our world. In this there is another lesson for us to discover.

Look again at Matthew 6:25, 28, 31. What did Jesus tell the people to avoid?

What are you worrying about today (or have you worried about recently)?

The places where we worry are the places where we need to learn to walk with God in greater confidence.

Read Psalm 139:23-24 in the margin. What is the prayer of the psalmist in these verses?

In verse 24, what does the psalmist ask God to do?

Why would worry offend God? Read Matthew 6:30 in the margin and write an explanation below.

23 Search me, O God, and know my heart; test me and know my anxious thoughts. 24 Point out anything in me that offends you, and lead me along the path of everlasting life. (Psalm 139:23-24)

"And if God cares so wonderfully for wildflowers that are here today and thrown into the fire tomorrow, he will certainly care for you. Why do you have so little faith?" (Matthew 6:30)

Throughout the Bible we see that God instructs people "do not be afraid" or "do not worry," and then God points to some aspect of His character as reinforcement of why worry isn't necessary. As we read in Psalm 19:1, the heavens are shouting to us of God's glory and power—in other words, God's got this! Know today that whatever it is you are facing in life, God's got it!

Live It Out

1. What is one thing that God impressed upon your heart during today's study?

2. Do you have a sense or leading from God about what you need to think or do differently as a result of what you've studied?

Talk with God

Do you really believe that God cares for all of the details of your life? What's on your heart today? Share that with God.

Day 5: Conforming Versus Transforming

Beauty Mark

As we live in holiness, God turns our hearts away from the world and toward Him.

Beauty Regimen

There are two ways that we live in this world: we *conform*, or we *transform*. I love how R. C. Sproul, in his classic book *The Holiness of God*, explains conforming versus transforming. The word *conform* means "with structure." When we conform, we go along with what's going on. In our beauty-conscious culture, conforming happens when we take our attitudes and beliefs from the world around us regarding what we should wear, how we should pose or act, or how we should interpret what we see in the mirror. When we conform, we chase the ideas of an elusive beauty that we all want to catch and claim. Even if we are not chasing beauty, we are secretly envious of the ones who are. Maybe we aren't trying because we don't think we can pull it off, so we're lamenting the fact that we'll never be *that* kind of beauty. However, when we infuse the pursuit of holiness into our lives, our focus shifts from conforming to transforming—from going with the crowd to moving in a new direction.[17] The Apostle Paul explains it in Romans 12:2:

> Don't copy the behavior and customs of this world, but let God transform you into a new person by changing the way you think. Then you will learn to know God's will for you, which is good and pleasing and perfect.

According to Romans 12:2, what is the evidence that we are conforming to this world?

What is the key to our transformation? How does God change us into new persons?

Read 2 Corinthians 5:17 in the margin. What act begins our transformation process?

When it comes to beauty, we move from conforming to transforming by allowing God to change the way we think about beauty. There are certain beauty myths that we discover are untrue, and as God transforms our minds, His truth integrates into our thinking. Here's another Scripture that shows how God wants to change the way we think.

This means that anyone who belongs to Christ has become a new person. The old life is gone; a new life has begun!
(2 Corinthians 5:17)

Look up Philippians 4:8 and fill in the blanks to indicate what God wants us to think about:

Instead of lies, fix your thoughts on what's _____.

Instead of what's dishonorable, fix your thoughts on what's
_____.

Instead of what's wrong, fix your thoughts on what's
_____.

Instead of lewd or impure things, fix your thoughts on what's
_____.

Instead of ugly or trashy things, fix your thoughts on what's
_____.

Instead of what's despicable or unworthy, fix your thoughts on what's _____.

Instead of what's inferior, fix your thoughts on what's
_____.

Instead of complaints, fix your thoughts on what's worthy of
_____.

Here's a story from a lovely Christian friend of mine who was brave enough to share her story about her ugly struggle with beauty:

I am thirty-one years old, and recently I married a wonderful man who tells me I am beautiful every day. It's tough for me to swallow at times. As a Christian, I know that God made me exactly the way I am, and that He thinks I am beautiful because I am His. But there is a disconnect between what I know and how I feel on a day-to-day basis. The older I become, the more I am aware of the fact that there are younger, cuter, more youthful girls out there that the world says are more beautiful than I am. I watch my weight constantly and monitor everything that goes in my mouth.

I have a hard time stepping out of the house without full hair and makeup. I scrutinize every imperfection on my face. I have long, full hair that other women compliment me on, but it's fake.

I shop a lot. I constantly size myself up against other women. It is honestly exhausting at times. I don't even know who I am dressing up for or trying to impress.

At this point, this is just my normal routine that I wouldn't know how to stop. I feel guilty, like I am perpetuating a spirit of comparison among women. But I don't really know where to draw the line between feeling good, having fun with beauty trends, and vanity.

I have an impressionable seven-year-old daughter and would like to break the trend so that she does not struggle with these same issues!

What are some of the challenges you face when it comes to changing your thoughts about the areas where you struggle with beauty?

Have you noticed any changes in your thinking since beginning this study?

Flip back through the past two weeks and write two Bible verses below that have made an impact on your thinking.

How have these verses challenged you?

You did it! Congratulations on completing this second week in our study. Understanding beauty from God's perspective can be a game-changer for how you think, feel, and live in regards to beauty. My sincerest prayer is that you are on your way to understanding more fully who God is and, as a result, understanding beauty from God's perspective. When we see how beautiful God is, we aren't tempted to settle for the cheap imitation of beauty that our world tries to offer us.

Live It Out

1. What is one thing that God impressed upon your heart during today's study?

2. Do you have a sense or leading from God about what you need to think or do differently as a result of what you've studied?

Talk with God

Use the two Bible verses you identified in your prayer time today. Trust that God wants to use His Word to change and transform your life. If you finish the prayer and sense a leading from God in any area of your life, write it below.

DEFINING DIVINE BEAUTY

The Hebrew word for good is *towb*, and the word means _____.

Beauty is _____ _____, not ours.

Beauty is a _____ _____.

Beauty is worthy of your _____ and best thinking because beauty is something that God deeply _____.

If we know _____ God is, then we will understand _____.

Divine Beauty – the _____, _____, and _____ nature of God.

Then God said, "Let us make human beings in our image, to be like us." (Genesis 1:26a)

You are beautiful because God created you.

But now you must be holy in everything you do, just as God who chose you is holy. For the Scriptures say, "You must be holy because I am holy." (1 Peter 1:15-16)

We have to realize that He is a holy God, and we are called to be holy as well—in our

_____, in our _____, and in our _____.

Week 3

CELEBRATING WHAT WE SEE

Memory Verse

"Seek the Kingdom of God above all else, and live righteously, and he will give you everything you need." (Matthew 6:33)

This Week's Theme
Seeking God first helps us reframe what we see in the mirror each day.

Give a woman a mirror and thirty seconds, and she'll tell you everything that is wrong with how she looks.

What do *you* focus on when you look in the mirror? Are you looking for wrinkles or checking to see if any roots are showing? Do you avoid the mirror altogether?

Every morning, I stumble into the bathroom to start my day. My first task is to conduct what I call my 101-point inspection of my face and body. Starting up top, I survey the landscape of my face, hair, and neck to see if any new lines, spots, wrinkles, or unwanted hair have appeared in places where they should not be. Then I turn sideways in the mirror to check whether my midsection looks thicker or thinner than the day before. I zero in on my lower stomach area because if something went wrong overnight, it's going to appear there first. Next, I'll swing my hips around to see if my rear-end has lowered any more since the day before. I admit there is no objective way to know for sure, but I check anyway.

The final phase of the inspection is the weigh-in. While many women avoid the scale, I invite this misery by stepping on the scale at least two or three times a week. There are rules to the weigh-in in order to make sure the weight registered is as low as possible. My most successful weigh-ins happen first thing in the morning, after I've used the restroom and, most important, when I am naked as a jaybird.

Whether you are a supermodel or you consider yourself closer to a frump, what you see in the mirror matters. I'm not trying to make a value statement about whether or not you should care about what you see; I'm just stating a fact. What you see isn't the most important thing about you, but *how* you see yourself does matter. Your interpretation of your reflection is inextricably linked to your emotions. When you feel good about what you see in the mirror, it has a positive impact on how you feel. Conversely, when you don't like what you see in the mirror, that also has an impact on how you feel.

So this isn't just about bemoaning your midsection or loathing your thighs. It's about the words you use to describe yourself: *ugly*, *fat*, *lazy*, *ashamed*, *depressed*, *sad*, *hopeless*. If we say these things to ourselves enough, we believe them. Once we believe them, it takes a lot to "un-believe" them, especially if we repeat these words to ourselves day after day.

What have you been saying to yourself in the mirror lately? Honey, listen to me: if Jesus were standing next to you as you look in the mirror, how would your conversation with yourself change? *Ouch!*

This week we'll learn how to celebrate what we see in the mirror. You'll learn how to shift your thoughts and feelings away from damaging, negative comments and, instead, focus on how God sees you—inside and out.

What you see [in the mirror] isn't the most important thing about you, but how you see yourself does matter.

Day 1: Seek God First— Identifying Your Mirrors

Beauty Mark

God's mirror must be the first mirror in our lives.

Beauty Regimen

Could you give up looking in the mirror? In her book *Mirror, Mirror Off the Wall*, sociologist Kjerstin Gruys tells the story of how she gave up looking in mirrors and other reflective surfaces for one year while she planned her wedding. Why? Her decision was motivated by the desire to save her self-esteem.

In previous years, Kjerstin overcame an eating discover. While shopping for wedding dresses, anxiety over her appearance resurfaced, and Kjerstin realized that she was falling back into old patterns of behavior. That's when she made a radical decision: she got rid of her mirrors at home.

At first it was difficult to avoid mirrors and other reflective surfaces. Getting a haircut was really tough! In time, Kjerstin adjusted and learned to avoid looking at herself in mirrors, relying instead on friends to provide feedback on her appearance. Of course, she knew that she might unintentionally catch a glimpse of her appearance. In a television interview conducted during the experiment, she admitted, "I do see myself out of the corner of my eye every day, because reflective surfaces are everywhere, but I don't look."[1]

On her wedding day, Kjerstin did her own makeup, but she still didn't look in the mirror.

At the end of the one-year experience, Kjerstin stood in front of a mirror that was filled with encouraging notes from her friends. She said that she liked what she saw and, even more, she felt that she was stronger. "It… opened up a new way of thinking about myself as a whole instead of just my looks."[2]

What do you think would happen if you stopped looking in the mirror for a year?

How would you manage getting dressed each day or styling your hair?

I don't know about you, but I think I could do it only if I could hire a hairdresser to come to my house each morning to do my hair. Otherwise, my hair would have its own story to tell by the end of that year!

Though Kjerstin eliminated physical mirrors, another kind of mirror took their place. While she avoided her image in traditional reflective mirrors, "mirrors" such as her fiancé and friends stepped into the gap to provide her with positive, affirming reflections of her shape, style, and soul.

When we look in a physical mirror, we capture a picture of what we see. Then we assign value to what we see—good or bad. If we allow others to act as mirrors for us, they capture a picture of what they see and then decide whether what they see is good or bad.

How does the concept of a mirror relate to our beauty narratives? Recall that our beauty narratives are stories we tell ourselves about our experiences with beauty. Those narratives are a collection of past events and experiences, whereas mirrors provide real-time feedback. How we manage the feedback our mirrors provide impacts the perspective and, ultimately, the trajectory of our beauty narrative. If we perceive the feedback as positive, then we will remember the image as positive—and vice versa.

Today, we're going to talk about how to prioritize the mirrors in our lives. Not all images are true images for us to believe. We're going to equip ourselves to focus only on the mirror that matters: God's mirror.

In the Walt Disney movie *Snow White and the Seven Dwarfs*, the Evil Queen appears in front of a magic mirror and asks this question:

"Magic mirror on the wall,
Who is the fairest one of all?"[3]

In some ways, we ask that question ourselves. We gaze in our bedroom or bathroom mirrors, and the spirit of that question floats in our subconscious—even though we ask it using different words:

Am I beautiful?
Am I enough?

If we aren't sure of the answer, we'll take a selfie with our phone and share the picture with social media. For most, asking "Am I beautiful?" is too frightening, but we're comfortable with asking, "How do I look?" We post our images, hoping that we receive the affirmation we feel we need. When our friends post their responses, they become our mirrors, creating a picture of us. Their comments help us decide whether or not we'll remember that image of ourselves in a positive or negative light.

There are a lot of different people in our lives serving as our mirrors. Here are a few categories of these human mirrors:

Funhouse Mirror

Feedback prompted by ever-changing cultural standards

Broken Mirror

Feedback provided in response to past images, causing pain and suffering

Honest Mirror

Feedback provided by those who love and care about you

Which mirrors influence you most these days?

How do you feel about that answer?

What are the positives and negatives associated with each of these three types of mirrors?

Funhouse Mirror

Broken Mirror

Honest Mirror

What if there was a giant mirror that we could look into to see ourselves in a way that reflects God's truth, goodness, and beauty in us? Lucky for us, that mirror exists!

Look up Matthew 6:33 and write the verse inside the mirror.

What are we to seek first before anything else?

Read Romans 14:17 in the margin. How does this verse explain the kingdom of God (what we are to seek)?

For the Kingdom of God is not a matter of what we eat or drink, but of living a life of goodness and peace and joy in the Holy Spirit. (Romans 14:17)

Extra Insight:

Humans cannot recognize themselves in a mirror until they are about eighteen months old.[4]

The original Greek word for "seek" is *zeteo*.[5] Seeking is serious business. It's more than just looking, as in looking for one's keys or an outfit to wear. In this case, seeking is a high-stakes pursuit of searching—the kind of searching a parent does when a child wanders off in the store. That's the kind of seeking that God wants us to do. We're not called to look for a casual connection with God. Rather, we're called to devote our effort and energy to connecting intimately with Him. At its essence, *zeteo* is an intense seeking with desire and purpose; therefore, "seek" means to desire or crave.

Seeking the kingdom of God means that we stop searching for approval from others or even for self-affirmation. Matthew 6:33 calls us to pursue God and His truth in whatever we think, say, or do, including when we look in the mirror or entertain feedback from other "mirrors" in our lives. Why?

First, because we're created *by* God and *in* the image of God, every time we look in the mirror is an opportunity for us to connect with God. Second, we are to seek and connect with God first because He knows that pursuing Him leads to deep and abiding satisfaction. God's truth about us remains, unlike the quickly dissolving nuggets of affirmation that people might provide.

According to Matthew 6:33 NIV, when are we to seek God?

F _ _ _ _

If we are going to claim victory over our ugly struggle with beauty, we must seek God *first*. When we seek God first, this means that we sift our opinions and beliefs about our bodies through the filter of God's truth and righteousness. Too often I allow my beliefs and life experiences to loom larger than God's sovereignty. When that happens, I'm calling my own shots. And that won't lead to victory.

Here's the story of a good friend of mine who applied Matthew 6:33 during a recent experience:

> While waiting for my mom to get a chest x-ray…there was a massive wall size mirror to my right. I glanced over and thought, "meh." Then I took a moment to really look at myself in the mirror. Not at the tee shirt, jeans, flip flops, or semi-brushed hair shoved back in a headband. But really look at myself. I saw one tired woman, I looked just run down, [even after losing over 100 pounds in the past year] I saw the rolls that were still there, loose skin on my upper arms, and all of my "flaws." I sighed deeply, closed my eyes, then looked again. [This time I thought] I'm an intelligent woman, I'm a child of God, I am a warrior. I will not let this mirror dictate how I feel about myself today or any other day.[6]

Disciplining ourselves to seek God first as we look in the mirror, rather than allow other mirrors to interpret how we think or feel about ourselves, will be tough. However, God calls us to make Him our top priority. When we seek the kingdom of God, we pursue a holy God who calls us to be holy, too.

On a scale of 1 ("not really") to 10 ("whole-heartedly"), how much are you prioritizing God in regards to your heart, mind, body, and soul?

What are the areas in your life where you are seeking God?

Read James 1:22-24 in the margin. What is the comparison James makes to explain what happens when we glance at God's truth but do not put it into practice?

> [22] But don't just listen to God's word. You must do what it says. Otherwise, you are only fooling yourselves. [23] For if you listen to the word and don't obey, it is like glancing at your face in a mirror. [24] You see yourself, walk away, and forget what you look like. (James 1:22-24)

God's Word is a mirror for us. When we study Scripture, we see ourselves as we really are: sinful, yet unconditionally loved. Yet when we neglect to seriously consider ourselves in the light of the Scripture, we lose the opportunity to see ourselves through God's righteous eyes. When we forfeit the chance to see ourselves as God sees us, we miss the chance for God to do the necessary work in us that leads to a life of goodness, peace, and joy. It's not enough for us to limit God's wisdom to just "spiritual" problems because God has a lot to say about every situation that we face in life as well as in the mirror.

Ladies, God knows us better than we could ever know ourselves. Whatever God calls us to do is for our best, both here on earth and for eternity. Seeking God first propels us toward a life of peace and joy.

Live It Out

1. What is one thing that God impressed upon your heart during today's study?

2. What do you sense God leading you to think or do differently as a result of what you've studied?

Talk with God

Every day we must choose to follow after God before anything else, including others' opinions that influence our thoughts or behaviors. Confess to God any places in your heart where He isn't first in your life. If there are influential "mirrors" that need to be removed, ask God for clarity and wisdom to let you know how to remove these mirrors in a way that honors God and does not harm others.

Day 2: See the Goodness, Blessing, and Purpose

Beauty Mark
You are God's masterpiece.

Beauty Regimen

Lizzie Velasquez was once labeled the "world's ugliest woman." She was born with a rare condition that prevents her from keeping or storing body fat. Now in her late twenties, Lizzie weighs less than seventy pounds and her skin hangs loose in many areas. She has limited vision and a weak immune system. According to Lizzie's website, there are only three other people in the world with a condition similar to hers.[7]

One day when she was a teenager, Lizzie was clicking through YouTube looking for some music. As she scanned through the column of related videos, she saw a video with a photo that looked really familiar. Imagine her surprise when she realized that she was the subject of a YouTube video. Lizzie says that her decision to watch the video was a "defining moment" in her life. She explains how she felt as she watched this eight-second video with no sound that labeled her the "world's ugliest woman" based on a photo taken when she was eleven years old: "I literally felt like somebody was putting their hand through the computer and punching me over and over and over."[8]

Lizzie saw that the video had been viewed by more than four million people and had thousands of comments, and she decided to read through every single one. And every single comment was negative. Many of the comments suggested that Lizzie walk around with a bag over her head or even kill herself. She explains what happened after she read the comments:

My confidence level went from being up here to being way down here to almost not even existent…In an instant it was brought down completely…I just wanted to make them feel bad…for hiding behind their computer screen and saying these awful things about someone they don't even know. But then I stopped and I realized, what am I going to accomplish?…I am going to be fighting a never-ending battle that's going to prove nothing.… But something clicked in me—some little voice in the back of my head, which I know was God. And I heard, "Just wait.… Just let it go and wait." [9]

By leaning on her faith, family, and friends, Lizzie made the decision to keep living and pursuing her goals and dreams. Rather than fight back, she moved forward and trusted God. Today Lizzie is the author of several books and a motivational speaker. She recognizes that the way God created her is in accordance with His perfect plan. She says:

My relationship with God was better than ever. Because in that moment when I realized that I wanted to be a speaker, I was like, "God, I get you now. I get it. I still have some questions, but I get it. You made me the girl that I am for a reason. You gave me all those struggles growing up to make me stronger. You made me look different so that I could see the beauty that isn't defined by the media." And yes, I am still learning, but the feeling that I get that I know that God is working through me and helping me tell you something is the greatest feeling in the entire world. [10]

I love Lizzie's story. She reminds us of how God truly sees us—as manifestations of His marvelous, perfect workmanship! When God sees you, He is not looking at your hips or your eyebrows. God sees your heart, your mind, your body, and your soul. Furthermore, God loves every part of you, even if you don't!

God wants us to shine as beacons on a hill. We are designed to radiate His truth and beauty to women in our world who are desperate to find a beauty that is pure and true. Yet, my friends, our God-given beauty cannot shine through if we are covering it up with bad attitudes or beliefs about ourselves. Our God-given beauty cannot shine through if we are carrying ourselves as if we are an afterthought—as if our bodies have not been specially designed for us.

Yesterday we discussed how we evaluate the different "mirrors" in our lives. Those mirrors are the real-time feedback filters that we use to judge whether or not we feel like enough in any given moment. However, the goal is for us to firmly plant ourselves in the reality that we are *always* enough, no matter what! Let's look at three steps that can move us toward this goal.

Step 1: See the Goodness

Read Genesis 1:26-28, 31. What did God proclaim once He reviewed all that He'd created, including humans?

If everything that God created is good, including humans, then why do we struggle to recognize God's goodness in our bodies? Check the reasons that describe your situation, or write your own response:

___ I struggle to see God's goodness in my body because of something I've done.

___ I struggle to see God's goodness in my body because of something devastating that happened to me.

___ I struggle to see God's goodness in my body because there are too many other powerful voices influencing my opinions of myself.

___ I struggle to see God's goodness in my body because I don't know how to see it.

___ Other: _____

In order for us to embrace God's goodness, we must believe that God is good and that His ultimate good is best for us.

Read Jeremiah 29:11 in the margin. What does this verse tell you about God's plan for you?

Think about Lizzie's story and how she recognized that a good God has a plan and purpose for her life. It's the same for you too! When you look at your body, you may feel that you're being held back because of what you see, but God's eyes aren't on your features; His eyes are on your future!

Let's take a moment and pray to God, acknowledging the goodness of our bodies. While you may not like the size or shape of one of your body parts, focus on the idea that this feature was created for you by God. Remember, everything that God made fits His definition of "goodness."

Fill in the blanks that follow. Then pray the completed paragraph as you look in the mirror:

God, thank You for my body, crafted by Your all-powerful, creative hands. Genesis 1:31 says that You have made all things good, including me. I reject every thought or belief that contradicts the reality of the marvelous workmanship of my physical being, including _____
_____. *Amen.*

Step 2: See the Blessing

When we recognize that we are blessed, we acknowledge God's kindness and provision. Unfortunately, we experience tremendous blessings all the time but fail to give God thanks.

If you've ever struggled with an illness or physical disability, you know the priceless value of a healthy body. Sadly, most of us take our bodies for granted. God knows what it took to create our complex human bodies, and He wants us not only to take care of them but also to recognize them as blessings.

If God is good, then everything that God creates must be good as well. Our bodies were not only created by a good God, but He also created our bodies to be good for us and to us.

Read Psalm 139:14 in the margin. Our bodies are described as:

w_____ c _____.

Our bodies give us the opportunity to move, create, connect, and so much more. List five things that your body has enabled you to do today that have blessed your life (give hugs, make food, etc.):

1.

2.

3.

4.

5.

It's important to take a moment and acknowledge how our divinely created bodies bless us.

Thank you for making me so wonderfully complex!
    Your workmanship is marvelous— how well I know it. (Psalm 139:14)

Extra Insight:

Facts about our unique human bodies:
1. As well as having unique fingerprints, humans also have unique tongue prints.
2. Our brains use 25 percent of the oxygen used by our bodies.
3. A human heart beats one hundred thousand times per day.
4. The smallest human bone is located in the middle ear. The stirrup bone is only 2.8 millimeters long.[11]

For we are God's masterpiece. He has created us anew in Christ Jesus, so we can do the good things he planned for us long ago. (Ephesians 2:10)

Fill in the blank below. Then grab that mirror again and pray the following aloud:

God, you've blessed me with this body. God, I struggle with _____
_____. Today I'm going
to honor this part of my body by remembering that You created it. Amen.

Step 3: See the Purpose

Each part of the human body has a God-defined purpose. We don't have to overthink this one, but we often condemn certain features of our bodies rather than give thanks for them. We are all unique creations, and God has a specific plan and purpose for our hearts, minds, bodies, and life experiences.

Read Ephesians 2:10 in the margin. Circle the words *masterpiece* and *good*. What role do our bodies play in God's purposes in this world?

It's time for us to stop focusing on our individual body parts and start recognizing our bodies as tools that God uses to bring glory to His name for the good of the people He calls us to serve.

Fill in the blanks below. Then grab that mirror one more time and pray the following:

God, it is so easy for me to say mean things in the mirror about my body. Instead, I recognize that You have a plan and purpose for my life. This means that I must look at my physical body as a tool You will use to make a difference in someone else's life.

Today, God, I will use

my mouth to _____,
my arms to _____,
my legs to _____, and
my feet to _____.

Live It Out

1. What is one thing that God impressed upon your heart during today's study?

2. What do you sense God leading you to think or do differently as a result of what you've studied?

Talk with God

Today you read three prayers that invited God to reshape how you see your body. With those prayers in mind, begin a new dialogue with God about any commitments that you need to make in order to continue to see the goodness, blessing, and purpose of your body.

Day 3: Celebrating the Many Colors of Beauty!

Beauty Mark
There is beauty in diversity.

Beauty Regimen

On lazy Sunday afternoons years ago, my husband and I loved watching painter Bob Ross on public television. In those days we'd coax our little ones down for an afternoon nap, and then we'd collapse on the sofa and let Bob's mellow voice soothe our tired bodies. Of course, watching Bob was predictable. We knew that he would paint a sky. Then there would be some type of lazy, winding river before the giant tree would anchor the landscape and end the thirty minutes of peaceful programming. Clearly, we didn't watch Bob and expect a cliffhanger: "Will he or won't he paint a tree? Come back next week!" Instead, we enjoyed how Bob worked his paint palette like a magician.

Before Bob's show, I never knew anything about colors such as yellow ocher, raw sienna, or titanium white. My youngest daughter is an emerging artist, so I see those colors now in her paint set; but back then those colors sounded foreign until we saw how mixing colors together could open up an entire new world of experiences to enjoy.

Bob loved trees. Watching Bob paint a tree gave me a sense of what it must have been like as God created the world with His incredible eye for beauty. Bob knew that while trees are brown, it takes layers of different color pigments to create a tree that would inspire a sleepy mom to stay awake a little longer. "Let's see," Bob would say. "We're going to take a little of this yellow ocher, a dab of this charcoal gray, and mix it with some of this burnt umber. Oh, that looks nice. I think it will look even better with a little of this titanium white."

At the end of each episode, I soaked up the multicolored layers of Bob's landscape. Each week he was able to create beauty because he understood how to combine colors to create harmony. Every color captured beauty because of the other colors surrounding it.

The human race portrays an equally stunning array of colors all throughout the world. Yet sadly, throughout history the most common color that has surfaced whenever different colors of humanity have come together is red—blood red.

As an African American woman writing about God, beauty, shame, and love, I have to talk about race. Yet I'm not talking about race in a way that divides. No politics or sweeping generalizations. My purpose in sharing about race is to lift up something that Jesus calls us to: *unity*. It is possible for us to enjoy our distinctive beauty and still find the beauty in one another whatever our skin color.

Join me as we dive into discovering why God created different skin colors as well as what we can learn from Scripture about how to relate to and love one another regardless of our skin color.

Read the following verses and write what each Scripture teaches about our differences and how we are to relate to one another:

Romans 10:12

1 John 2:9-11

Genesis 1:27

John 13:34

1 Corinthians 12:12-13

Our comfort level with the topic of race often depends on our background and life experience. When are you comfortable talking about race? When do you become uncomfortable?

What was your experience with race growing up?

How have your early experiences with race impacted your life as an adult?

Race is one of the most controversial issues in our society. That's not news. It is embarrassing to know that as Christians, we bear some shameful race-related history. Unfortunately, through the centuries Christians and other religious groups have used the Bible to justify the mistreatment of different racial groups.

What does Romans 2:11 tell us?

Since we're human, we naturally gravitate to people who look or sound like us. Yet God doesn't show favoritism. Unfortunately, not all Christians and churches have a great reputation for accepting people as they are.

What is the impact on the gospel message when people in the church do not see other races and cultures as Jesus does?

There was a time in our human history when dark-skinned people were believed to be cursed based on an account recorded in Genesis 9. This belief was used to justify many hurtful things, including slavery.

What was this curse about? It goes back to an incident involving Noah. After the Great Flood that destroyed all of the earth's inhabitants except for Noah and his family, God instructed Noah to set about the process of rebuilding their lives on earth. At one point, Noah drank too much and passed out naked. Noah's dark-skinned son, Ham, didn't handle his father's drunken condition properly. Noah became very angry and issued a curse that day.

Read Genesis 9:25-27. Who was cursed?

Who wasn't cursed?

Noah's curse creates many questions. What did Ham do wrong? Why did Noah curse Ham's son, Canaan, instead of Ham? Were all dark-skinned people cursed because of Ham's actions?

The Bible gives us answers to some of these questions, but a few remain unanswered. First, when Ham discovered his father's nakedness, the prudent thing to do was to cover Noah's exposed body. Rather, Ham went out to tell his brothers about their father's condition. When Noah awoke, his anger was apparent, and Noah cursed Canaan, one of Ham's four sons. There's still some question as to why the curse on Canaan wasn't experienced at that time, but we see later in the Old Testament that Canaan's descendants were conquered by the Israelites when they entered the Promised Land.

Unfortunately, the story of Noah and his sons became a common justification for religiously endorsed slavery, even though that is a misinterpretation of Scripture. Pastor Tony Evans lifts up some of the reasons why this incident should not have been used as an argument for slavery:

1. The Bible limits curses to three or four generations (Exodus 20:5);
2. Canaan's brothers—Cush, Mizraim, and Put—became the progenitors of national peoples who continue today in Ethiopia, Egypt, and Libya; and
3. in Exodus 20:6, God says that curses based on disobedience are reversed when people turn back to obedience.[12]

What are your thoughts about the story of Noah and his sons and how that story was used to justify slavery?

Whenever I see someone who looks different from me and I'm tempted to think I am better than that person—whether it's because I'm dressed better, I'm taller, or I'm more attractive or intelligent (none of us is exempt from this human tendency)—there's something that I do. It's called the "Jesus Exercise," and it's very simple. I look the person directly in the eyes and whisper very quietly one single word: "Jesus." Now, they cannot hear me say it (that would be weird), but repeating Jesus' name is a verbal cue to remind me that the person before me was made in the image of God. Not only that, but Jesus died for this person just as He died for me, and in God's eyes our value is the same.

Read Ephesians 2:14-15 in the margin. What did Jesus bring? How did he do it?

Why is unity so important?

What impact could we, the church, have in our world if we were to truly love and care for everyone, no matter their race, color, or culture?

Let's be honest. We've *all* thought that we are better than someone. While it doesn't always feel safe to do so, I believe that there are occasions when racial healing could occur if we would acknowledge our individual prejudice. We cannot experience the totality of beauty if we hold on to our prejudice. You and I have to challenge those preformed negative thoughts. How can we do that?

1. *Acknowledge it.* What are the people and places where you either experience the "at-least-I'm-not-like-them" feeling or the "they-make-me-feel-uncomfortable-or-afraid" feeling?

[14] For Christ himself has brought peace to us. He united Jews and Gentiles into one people when, in his own body on the cross, he broke down the wall of hostility that separated us. [15] He did this by ending the system of law with its commandments and regulations. He made peace between Jews and Gentiles by creating in himself one new people from the two groups. (Ephesians 2:14-15)

2. *Talk about it.* Yes, our world doesn't make it easy to talk about race, but I encourage you to start with someone who is trustworthy. Try this: "I am struggling with (insert specific situation), and I need to talk about it." Be honest with one person, and go from there.

I want to commend you for completing today's study. Engaging in discussion about race is difficult for everyone. However, Jesus brought peace and unity to the human race through His death on the cross and His resurrection. In Jesus, we are one! And there is great beauty in our unity!

Live It Out

1. What is one thing that God impressed upon your heart during today's study?

2. What do you sense God leading you to think or do differently as a result of what you've studied?

Talk with God

Invite God to reveal your own prejudices about others. Then ask God to create opportunities for you to connect with women who are different from you, including women of other races, so that you might build relationships with those sisters in Christ.

Day 4: You Are Always God's Number One Pick!

Beauty Mark
God always chooses us.

Beauty Regimen

Esther is my favorite figure in the Bible. Her attitude, beliefs, and character demonstrate the ideal balance of inner and physical beauty. The snapshot of her life story rests about halfway through the Old Testament.

Within the ten chapters of this epic saga of mystery, betrayal, and eventual triumph, we see how God uses Esther's inner and physical beauty to save the lives of His chosen people, the Israelites. Her story demonstrates how God's purpose unfolds behind the scenes in all of our lives as He works all things out for His and our ultimate good.

While all cultures, both ancient and contemporary, reward beautiful women in many tangible ways, physical beauty always comes with a cost. In Esther's case, her emerging beauty captured the attention of the king's staff, who were commanded to sweep the city and bring back beautiful young women for the king. The previous queen had disrespected her husband, so her crown was removed and the search for a new queen had begun.

The second chapter of Esther's story documents the process of preparing these young women to meet the king. Since the king was the top man in the land, his staff prepared the women to meet the king's high standards. We might be shocked at the lengths that celebrities employ to look glamorous, but many of their strategies could be considered elementary compared to what Esther and the other candidates experienced. Some of those beauty treatments included six months of massages with oil and six months of cosmetic treatments. Now, I think that after twelve months of daily spa treatments and the best foods, I'd probably look pretty good. What about you?

We don't know how Esther felt about being taken from her home and entered into an ancient Persian version of *The Bachelor*, but we do know that Esther's uncle Mordecai told the young girl to keep her Jewish heritage hidden. Chances are that Esther felt uncertain. She had been taken from two homes at a young age—first her parents' and now her uncle's—and now she was living with a group of women who were in the running to be queen. Only one would be chosen.

If you've read Esther's story, you know that the king chose her to become queen of Persia. Esther got the crown, the clothes, fancy horses, and a wing in the palace.

The thrill of getting chosen is directly related to what one is being chosen for. When women receive a rose on the television show *The Bachelor*, the thrill of being chosen is short-lived. Why? Because the women know that their chosen status lasts for a brief period of time.

If being chosen has an expiration date, then is being chosen really worth it? Our culture seems to think so. Countless ordinary people have grabbed their fifteen minutes of fame and stretched them as long as possible. Reality television shows have created the illusion that regular people can be famous, popular, and wealthy just like bona fide celebrities. But for how long? And at what price?

Let's take a look at what it means for God to choose us now and forever.

There once was a man named Jacob whose life is recorded in Scripture. I must admit that I struggle with Jacob's story. He wasn't always a stand-up

"What's more, I am with you, and I will protect you wherever you go. One day I will bring you back to this land. I will not leave you until I have finished giving you everything I have promised you." (Genesis 28:15)

guy. In fact, Jacob's name means "deceiver." Not only did he take advantage of his twin brother, Esau, and steal his inheritance, but he also gained the all-important appointment as spiritual leader of the entire family once their father, Isaac, passed away. Through trickery, Jacob secured wealth and influence.

From my human perspective, Jacob shouldn't have been entitled to blessings from God after this behavior. Only stand-up people should have good things happen in their lives, right? Apparently God has a different viewpoint.

There came a point in Jacob's life when he needed to leave home. First, Esau was angry over the lost blessing and inheritance, and Jacob feared revenge. Additionally, Jacob was also looking for a wife. However, his family was living in a foreign land, and Jacob was forbidden to marry the women in that land. As a result of both situations, Jacob's father, Isaac, sent Jacob to an uncle's house to find a wife.

One night during Jacob's journey, God appeared to him in a dream. Identifying Himself by using the word LORD or "sacred one," God then proclaimed a special promise or covenant to Jacob. Echoing an earlier covenant with Abraham that his lineage would be as numerous as the stars in sky, God promised Jacob that his descendants would own the land where Jacob was sleeping and that they would spread out across the earth.

Read Genesis 28:15 in the margin. What is the promise that God makes to Jacob?

Can you recall a situation when you sensed God's enduring presence? If so, how did God's presence comfort or guide you?

In that moment, Jacob realized that he was chosen by God for a special reason. Jacob didn't do anything to deserve being chosen; God simply chose him. Even better, God promised to stick with him and not abandon him.

Did you know that God chooses you? You look in the mirror and see your wrong choices, awful mistakes, shortcomings, or bad behavior, but God still chooses you. Even if you look in the mirror and see only a woman who has been brutally victimized by others, God still chooses you. He always has. Too often we let our life circumstances convince us that He doesn't care. But even when we reject God, He still chooses us.

What are some times when we women long to be chosen?

What are some of the ugly consequences that can happen when we aren't chosen? How do we sometimes respond?

What does it mean to you that God has chosen you? To what extent do you believe this is true?

Read Hebrews 13:5b in the margin. What promise does God make to us?

"For the LORD
your God is living
among you.
He is a mighty
savior.
He will take delight
in you with gladness.
With his love,
he will calm all
your fears.
He will rejoice
over you with
joyful songs."
(Zephaniah 3:17)

Our greatest fear in life is rejection, the horrific sensation that we are not good enough to be loved. This becomes a particularly sensitive area for single women who desire to find love, companionship, and marriage. But we all struggle with the fear of rejection at various times and in various ways. This fear is amplified when we think that rejection is our fault because of how we look.

When someone is with us, that means something! Walking shoulder-to-shoulder with someone evokes confidence and the feeling that we are not alone.

Read Zephaniah 3:17 in the margin. In this verse, God is responsible for the action and His people are the recipients of the action. What does it say that God will do?

How could being more connected to God alleviate your fears of loneliness or rejection?

The next time that you are feeling lonely or unloved, instead of thinking about why you might have been rejected by others, think about a God who makes you His number one pick every single time.

Live It Out

1. What is one thing that God impressed upon your heart during today's study?

2. What do you sense God leading you to think or do differently as a result of what you've studied?

Talk with God

If your self-esteem or self-image has been beaten down because you've been passed over too many times, today is the day to lay down those feelings of inadequacies or failures. Bring those memories and feelings to God in prayer. Open your hands, release those hurts to Him, and claim the peace and freedom that God alone can provide.

Day 5: A Great Reminder for Those Really Bad Days!

Beauty Mark
In God's eyes, you are always enough.

Beauty Regimen

I love cookies! Not as much as I love Jesus, my husband, or my kids, but I totally love them—about as much as my favorite pair of shoes. However, my love of cookies is a double-edged sword. As much as I love them, they also betray me.

It began innocently one afternoon at the grocery store. I strolled through the bakery section on my way to the produce section when I saw the magic orange markdown sticker. Why do they make those stickers neon orange? So that I could see them a half-mile away! I wheeled my cart toward that pyramid of special bargains and discovered sale-priced gourmet cookies of all flavors and kinds. I snatched up a box of white chocolate macadamia nut cookies. By the way, these were the good kind—made with lots of macadamia nuts, not just half a nut per cookie like the cheap ones.

When I returned home, I promised myself that I would eat only one cookie. I checked the nutrition information, and at almost three hundred calories per cookie, restraint was required. Except I didn't show restraint. One cookie tasted so good that I ate another. Then I hid the box from plain view. That totally did not work! I grabbed another cookie. By the third cookie in an hour, my soul knew that I was out of control, but mercy help me, I ate a fourth cookie! Thank goodness that there were only six cookies in the box. I gobbled down five cookies. Oh, they tasted so good in my mouth, but the euphoria quickly died as my mind started to reconcile the damage that had been done.

Five cookies! What were you thinking?

Now, I know that these were just cookies. But they are a small example of a time when I beat myself up for behavior that didn't meet my expectation. We all make mistakes. Unfortunately, we've become professional fighters when it comes to *our* mistakes. We've got a gold belt in the art of beating ourselves up.

Many of you feel guilt or shame because you believe that you've made bad choices with your body—whether you've overeaten, neglected or abused your body, or allowed others to misuse you. Furthermore, some of you feel that you can't turn things around. So we do the only thing we know we won't fail at: we beat ourselves up.

Here are a few quotes from the *Created with Curves* survey I've mentioned previously:

> "I've let myself go."
> "My body is messed up because I…"
> "I abuse my body because it was abused by someone else."
> "I've stretched my body by overeating."

As we beat ourselves up with words or thoughts or lack of self-care, we heap shame on ourselves, hoping that we will change if we feel bad enough about our behavior. Here is an important truth: shame doesn't work. Shaming yourself never creates lasting, positive results. Shame can jump-start a behavior change, but it cannot sustain it. Shame or embarrassment can drive us to throw on the brakes, but moving forward in shame or embarrassment is painful; and we do not thrive that way.

Stop blaming yourself for what you've allowed to happen. Whether it's gaining weight, letting your appearance go, or allowing yourself to become bitter, shame isn't going to dig you out of the hole.

Furthermore, when we blame ourselves for behavior that we think we should be able to control, then we can't love ourselves. When this happens, we start thinking that maybe God can't love us either because we have failed in some area of our lives.

Beautiful friend, when God's gaze falls on you, there is only love. God knows your entire story. He knows the moments of pain or horror tucked silently deep within your heart.

Let's look at a series of verses in Scripture that reminds us we are always enough, even when we make mistakes.

Read Psalm 139:17-18 below:

How precious are your thoughts about me, O God.
   They cannot be numbered!
I can't even count them;
   they outnumber the grains of sand!

Circle the word *precious* **and underline the phrase "your thoughts about me." Then draw an arrow from the circle to the underlined phrase.**

The word *precious* also alludes to *vast* thoughts. This means that our omniscient God has lots and lots of wonderful thoughts about each of us individually. You and I are constantly on God's radar, and that's a good thing!

Yet when we mess up and live in the Land of Shame, our inclination is to hide from God.

When you mess up, how do you think God really feels about you in that moment?

Read Jeremiah 31:3 in the margin. Then rewrite the verse below, replacing "my people" with your name.

I get tingly inside when I read these words and soak them in because they remind me of this well-worn statement: *There is nothing we can do to make God love us more, and there is nothing we can do to make God love us less.*

How hard or easy is it for you to embrace that you are loved unconditionally by God, no matter what? Why?

Read Lamentations 3:21-23 in the margin. What do these verses tell us about God's love and mercy?

21 Yet I still dare to hope
   when I remember this:
22 The faithful love of the LORD never ends!
   His mercies never cease.
23 Great is his faithfulness;
   his mercies begin afresh each morning.
(Lamentations 3:21-23)

When you think about God's mercy being renewed each morning in your life, how can that bring you hope when you make mistakes?

Look up Romans 8:1 and write it below:

Condemnation feels like a heavy, leaded blanket. It wraps around our bodies and weighs us down. Are you carrying a blanket of condemnation? If so, you can toss that blanket on the ground. Where there is condemnation, there is no hope. But Jesus Christ is the hope of the world!

Romans 8:1 contains a promise that is accessible to those of us who have placed our faith in Jesus Christ. This is an important truth to remember as we look in the mirror each day. We look at our faces and see the history of our decisions, both good and bad. In our eyes we see memories of circumstances and situations—some that were in our control and some that were not. In that mirror, we look into the face of one who knows everything about us. It's also the face of one who is quick to condemn.

Here's a story from one of the women who took the *Created with Curves* survey who is learning to love, not condemn, herself:

I have struggled with my weight since I was a child. As a kindergartner, I weighed in at seventy pounds. I have never seen anything less than plus-sized clothing. When I was nineteen, I was at the smallest weight of my life, a size 16/18 pants. I loved the way I felt. Then I became pregnant, and I am now at the heaviest weight I have ever been.

I do not pity myself much anymore. I have been immersing myself in challenging Bible studies and realize that God loves me no matter what. Now I am learning to love myself, because I will keep abusing a body that I do not love.

I have noticed that I am invisible. I work in an office, and people literally look past me as if I am not even there. I have received looks of pure disgust from men and women, and people go around me as if I will make them fat just by being in their air space. The opportunities that are prevalent in the company are presented first to those who are thinner than me, yet nothing stings more than the mental war.

These things hurt, and I keep close to the Lord during the various daily battles I face.

What has helped this woman to break free from self-condemnation?

I know there are many times when I need to lean into the words of Romans 8:1, wrapping them around my heart to protect it from my stinging condemnation. Even if what you are struggling with isn't your fault, you have to fight against the self-condemning thoughts that you should have been stronger or that you should have stopped what happened. Always remember this: if you are in Christ, God doesn't condemn you, no matter what the face in the mirror wants you to believe.

Live It Out

1. What is one thing that God impressed upon your heart during today's study?

2. What do you sense God leading you to think or do differently as a result of what you've studied?

Talk with God

What do you need to let go of once and for all? Is it a memory or painful experience that you've continued to carry even though you've tried to put it out of your heart and mind? Pick a Scripture from today's study, such as Lamentations 3:21-23 or Romans 8:1, and use it as your prayer today. Pray until you sense that coat of condemnation falling from your body and God's forgiveness replacing it.

CELEBRATING WHAT WE SEE

Sometimes our greatest fear is that we are not _____.

There are times when we look in the mirror for whatever we can find to

_____ that fear.

"_____ the Kingdom of God above all else, and live righteously, and he will give you everything you need." (Matthew 6:33)

Seeking God means that we are _____ God above all things, including what we see in the mirror.

When we see God first, there are three things we can choose to see:

1. See the _____.
God's goodness is in us.

Then God looked over all he had made, and he saw that it was very good!
And evening passed and morning came, marking the sixth day.
(Genesis 1:31)

2. See the _____.
Our bodies are a blessing, not a burden.

You made all the delicate, inner parts of my body
        and knit me together in my mother's womb.
Thank you for making me so wonderfully complex!
        Your workmanship is marvelous—how well I know it.
                (Psalm 139:13-14)

3. See the _____.
Each of us has a unique purpose.

For we are God's masterpiece. He has created us anew in Christ Jesus, so we can do the good things he planned for us long ago.

(Ephesians 2:10)

Week 4

GENTLE AND QUIET BEAUTY

Memory Verse

You should clothe yourselves instead with the beauty that comes from within, the unfading beauty of a gentle and quiet spirit, which is so precious to God. (1 Peter 3:4)

This Week's Theme
True beauty flows from the inside out.

Have you ever run into a woman who was bad-tempered, rude, or argumentative? What about a woman who complains all of the time or is greedy? It doesn't matter what that woman looks like on the outside; you don't want to be anywhere near her. Sometimes I am that cranky, bad-tempered woman. I don't want to be, but I can be. And there's nothing beautiful about me in those moments. In fact, I'm downright ugly at those times.

In contrast, a kind, compassionate, and humble woman is like honey. Her sweet disposition will draw anyone and everyone to her. People will seek her out, and she will be valued for how good she makes them feel about being with her. No matter her physical appearance, her inner qualities leave an imprint on others' souls that is far deeper than the visual impression she would make on their eyes. Ultimately, she's the kind of woman who gives us women a great name.

My friends, your inner beauty is the light that our dark world desperately needs. This God-cultivated beauty will draw people to you like moths to a flame. While things never end well for a moth drawn to a flame, those who are drawn to your God-inspired inner beauty will want to know where your radiance comes from. In that moment, you will have a platform to share about your God-given beauty and invite others to experience the same.

This week we will unpack the specific qualities of inner beauty.

> ³ Don't be concerned about the outward beauty of fancy hairstyles, expensive jewelry, or beautiful clothes. ⁴ You should clothe yourselves instead with the beauty that comes from within, the unfading beauty of a gentle and quiet spirit, which is so precious to God.
>
> (1 Peter 3:3-4)

Beauty Mark

Inner beauty flows from a gentle and quiet spirit.

Beauty Regimen

Have you noticed the number of reality television shows that feature beautiful women behaving badly? There are too many shows to list! The premier episode usually begins with gorgeous women with long, flowing hair, air-brushed makeup, stiletto-length eyelashes, and stunning designer clothes. However, it doesn't take long before the women begin to fight, argue, scheme, and plot against one another or try to ensnare some unsuspecting bystander into one of their jealous plots. While I may not watch the actual shows, I see the weekly teasers on television or online, showing snippets of upcoming episodes featuring ugly words, horrible drama, nasty arguments, or violent fighting. Audiences everywhere tune in each week to watch physically beautiful women saying and doing horrible, ugly things. Does the fact that they fit our culture's definition of physical beauty excuse these women from what comes out of their hearts and minds?

I'm not planning on starring on any reality shows, but occasionally some of the sinful crud that's stuck in my heart and mind comes out of my mouth. In those moments, I'm pretty ugly, and there's no amount of makeup that can cover up that kind of ugly.

It's time for us to unpack the specific qualities of inner beauty. We're also going to discuss why and how we can apply these qualities in our lives. The main framework for defining inner beauty is explained by one of Jesus' disciples, Peter.

Read 1 Peter 3:3-4 in the margin. What kind of beauty did Peter want the women to cultivate?

Why would Peter describe the qualities of inner beauty as "unfading"? What gives them eternal staying power?

Did Peter ban or condemn expensive or nice jewelry or clothing?

Ladies, you don't have to pack up your nice clothes or cute shoes and give them away. Peter isn't condemning jewelry or makeup. In contrast to a facade-obsessed culture, Peter redirects our pursuit of physical beauty to inner beauty and defines the hallmarks of inner beauty: a gentle and quiet spirit.

So what is a "gentle and quiet spirit"? If we take the words at face value without understanding the biblical context, we may miss the real meaning of the words.

Read my definitions of gentleness and quietness in the sidebar. Notice how these inward qualities show up in our outward behaviors toward others. A woman with a gentle and quiet spirit isn't a weak wallflower. In fact, she's quite the opposite!

The unfading beauty of a gentle and quiet spirit attracts and blesses because this is a woman who is others-focused rather than self-centered or inward-focused.

How would you define a gentle and quiet spirit in your own words?

There is nothing small or quiet about me. Everything about me, as my Spanish-speaking friends say, *es grande*. I'm 5'10" with big feet and a loud voice. So in the past, whenever someone would teach about gentle and quiet beauty, I would feel less than in comparison with women who appeared demure and agreeable.

At many points in life, I believed that soft-spoken, reserved women were the ideal Christian women. I thought that these women never felt the need to express an opinion and were content standing in the background. They never raised their voices and had never-ending smiles on their faces. They exuded "gentle" and "quiet" with a seemingly natural ease, and I did not. How could it be so unnatural for me? I felt like a failure.

Then I studied and discovered the true meaning of "a gentle and quiet spirit." I exhaled with relief! It is possible for me to be demonstrative yet still reflect the "gentle and quiet spirit" that supports God's framework for a woman's beautiful nature.

When I discovered the meaning of the original words, my first thought was, *I can do that!* I discovered that instead of needing to be a shy wallflower with no opinions, God's prescription for inner beauty is a mixture of qualities that can complement even a girl like me. Of course, I couldn't

Extra Insight:

Gentleness: Maintaining a gracious attitude, friendly behavior, and humble character.

Quietness: Choosing to possess tranquillity, respect, and submissiveness over worry or rebelliousness.

³ Don't be selfish; don't try to impress others. Be humble, thinking of others as better than yourselves. ⁴ Don't look out only for your own interests, but take an interest in others, too. (Philippians 2:3-4)

achieve this inner beauty on my own, but I had confidence that God would guide me to it.

The pursuit of inner beauty is often the place where God and I meet to do business.

When it comes to nurturing gentleness, 1 Corinthians 13:4-5 holds some practical advice. Look up that verse and write below, substituting your name in place of the word *love*.

Now, circle the words or phrases in 1 Corinthians 13:4-5 indicating the qualities you are living out, and underline those that you need to improve upon.

Look back at the definition of quietness in the margin on page 101. In your life, what are some of the obstacles that get in the way of developing quietness?

In addition to exterior obstacles to quietness, there are interior ones as well. I must remember that some of my ugliest moments happen when my words and attitude don't reflect an unfading, gentle, and quiet beauty. In those moments when I fight to be right, when I choose to worry instead of patiently wait, or when I offend instead of reflect, I am allowing the ugliness of sin to rise to the surface.

List a woman in your life who exemplifies a gentle and quiet spirit. What can you learn from her that you can apply in your own life?

Read Philippians 2:3-4 in the margin. What do these verses have in common with cultivating a gentle and quiet spirit?

There's another passage of Scripture that complements the goal of cultivating inner beauty as defined by a gentle and quiet spirit.

Read Galatians 5:22-23. How would you divide the fruit of the Spirit according to the qualities of gentleness and quietness?

Gentleness   **Quietness**

One of the most controversial aspects of quietness is submission, or the "action of accepting or yielding…to the will or authority of another person."[1] Submission is a choice. If you are forced to comply or yield, that is not submission. God's established order for humanity means that there are certain times and situations when others are in authority over us or in positions or relationships deserving mutual submission.

If I'm at work and my boss asks me to handle a task, I have a choice about whether or not I will follow his instructions. I also have a choice about the attitude that I will display while following those instructions. A contrary, belligerent, or rebellious heart not only creates tension within our relationships but also twists and ties our emotions (and our facial features).

Submission is about trust. When we submit, we recognize that we don't always have to be right and we don't always have to have our way. God is in charge of all of the details of our lives—over and above those of everyone else. When we show respect and deference to others, we are ultimately submitting to God.

And when we submit to the authority of an all-knowing, all-powerful, ever-present Creator God, we possess a beautiful tranquillity and peace because we don't have to worry about anything. We are confident that He will take care of us.

Where are the places or relationships in your life where you may need to demonstrate submission?

What feels threatening about submission?

How do you think your desire to cultivate inner beauty will be impacted if you shy away from submission?

Complete the following:

I display a *gentle spirit* when:

I display a *quiet spirit* when:

What is your most significant challenge when it comes to cultivating a gentle and quiet spirit?

As we close today's lesson, I'll leave you with a practical exercise that can help you to overcome challenges as you seek to cultivate a gentle and quiet spirit. Look at yourself in the mirror as you imagine and roleplay conversations with your friends, family, coworkers, or others. Pay attention to the words that you use and how your face looks when you use those words. If necessary, record yourself speaking and evaluate the hardness or softness of your tone. Perhaps there are certain words or phrases you need to eliminate from your vocabulary, especially if those words are contrary to the definition of gentleness. Ladies, our greatest desire should be to let our inner beauty shine through. Therefore, this exercise will help you see any adjustments that you can make to your face or tone when communicating.

Live It Out

1. What is one thing that God impressed upon your heart during today's study?

2. What do you sense God leading you to think or do differently as a result of what you've studied?

Talk with God

As you wrap up today, ask God to bring to mind any places or relationships where you need to cultivate a gentle and quiet spirit, as well as specific individuals you might consider apologizing to if you have been unkind or rude.

Day 2: Standing Tall

Beauty Mark
God's Word strengthens us with strong roots.

Beauty Regimen

The great fear of my paternal grandmother, Helen Violet Reed, was that her granddaughters would be tall. At 5'8", Mama, as we called her, grew up under tremendous Southern scrutiny for her height. In her eyes, a proper woman simply could not be tall. When I got older, I realized Mama didn't want her granddaughters to endure the stares and comments she suffered during her younger years.

By the time I was eleven years old, I towered over my other female cousin, Lynn. Mama often vocalized her concerns: "Oh, Barbara," she would say, "I hope you don't grow to be as tall as I am." Well, that hope turned to heartache for Mama because I didn't stop growing until I reached 5'10" as a junior in high school.

While she never explained why being tall was a bad thing, Mama decided to help her gangly granddaughter make the best of the situation.

One summer afternoon, she positioned a hardcover book on top of my head and said, "Now walk." She ordered me to walk down the length of her living room with that book on my head. For the first few days, that book spent more time on the floor than atop my head. But Mama sat in her chair and repeated, "Barbara, pick it up and try again."

She wanted me to learn how to walk and stand tall.

Before that summer, I slouched my shoulders all of the time. Not only was I tall but I was also shy. Being tall drew unwanted attention. Furthermore, my friends were much shorter than me, so I walked with my head down and shoulders slumped over because I felt so oversized.

Mama and that hardcover book trained my body to stand straight and tall. With the book on my head, I couldn't hold my head too high or too low. Instead, my shoulders had to be slightly back and my neck had to be strong for my head to stay steady and keep the book from falling.

A first-born perfectionist, I practiced until that book stayed on my head and I could walk and turn with ease. The more that book stayed on my head, the more confident that I felt. Every time I crossed the floor without the book falling, there was a little voice in my head that sounded a lot like the engine from the story "The Little Engine That Could," saying, "I think I can, I think I can."

My posture is often the first thing people notice about me; I couldn't have bad posture if I tried. I will always be grateful for the lessons my grandmother taught me that summer. I learned how to stand tall, which I recognize is a gift that should never be taken for granted. Yet it would take a few more decades for me to learn how to stand tall spiritually.

Today we're going to discuss what it means to develop strong roots. It won't mean much if we win our ugly struggle with beauty now only to fall apart all over again in the future. We want to develop strong roots to hold us stable no matter the way that the winds of our culture blow.

In 1991, a tree named the Dyerville Giant toppled to the ground. The more than 350-foot-tall California tree is said to have been about two thousand years old. Why did the great tree fall? Though heavy rains were a factor in saturating and loosening the soil, root rot was discovered once the base was exposed. It would seem that after decades of tourists walking over the tree's shallow roots, the root system weakened to the point that it couldn't support itself, and the mighty tree toppled over with a nudge from a neighboring tree.[2]

A tree cannot survive without a healthy root system taking in nourishment from the soil and anchoring it deep in the ground. When a tree's root system fails, it's just a matter of time before the tree can no longer stand tall. Its support system becomes too weak to keep it upright.

At times, different circumstances in life rush at us and make us feel like we might topple over like the Dyerville Giant—especially when it comes to beauty. Someone says something hurtful or we have a painful experience, and we feel like we want to collapse on the ground and die. Is it difficult for us to stand tall, hold our heads up high, and maintain our God-given gift of beauty in a world that wants to destroy that gift? Yes! If we expect to stand tall, we must have strong roots holding us up.

Have you ever noticed how often the Bible compares us to trees? In the Scriptures, trees are often used as a symbol to describe our faith or strength.

Read the verses below and write the quality of faith that each describes.

Psalm 1:3

Proverbs 3:18

Matthew 7:17-19

Psalm 92:12

Think about a tree with a strong root system. It survives temperature changes, animals, insects, droughts, and floods, yet it survives. A tree doesn't rely on other trees to prop it up; it stands or falls based on the integrity and stability of its roots. The quality and amount of fruit a tree produces depends on strength of the foundation of the tree. The same goes for you and me.

Read Colossians 2:7 in the margin. Circle the word *roots* and draw an arrow from that word to the word *him*. Then read the definition of taproot in the margin. As Christians, who is our taproot?

Roots are a metaphor for our faith. The strength of our faith directly correlates to how we will manage our beauty narratives, as well as how we will allow culture to influence our ideas about beauty. The depth of our faith also correlates to the long-term resiliency that we display when faced with challenges or hardships.

Roots originate from the taproot of the plant. A single, original main root makes the other roots possible. The same goes for us spiritually. Salvation through Jesus Christ makes our faith possible. There is no faith without Christ. We can't pursue strong roots unless we start with Christ.

Let your roots grow down into him [Christ], and let your lives be built on him. Then your faith will grow strong in the truth you were taught, and you will overflow with thankfulness. (Colossians 2:7)

Extra Insight:

Taproot:
The large main root of a plant from which smaller roots grow.[3]

At what point did you place your faith in Jesus Christ? Summarize your spiritual journey to salvation by answering these three questions:

1. What was your life like before you asked Jesus Christ to be your Savior?

2. When did you become aware that you needed a Savior?

3. How has your life been since accepting Jesus Christ as your Savior?

Look at Colossians 2:7 again. The Apostle Paul switches from talking about roots to foundations. Colossian 2:7 instructs us to build our lives on Christ. I describe our foundation of faith as the ABCs:

Attitude: Living out a heart-desire to love God and love others

Beliefs: Living out the conviction to follow and obey God's Word

Character: Living out Christ-centered moral qualities

On a scale of 1 (not at all) to 10 (absolutely), how would you rate your current development of your ABCs of faith?

____ Attitude   ____ Beliefs   ____ Character

What are some specific areas in your development of the ABCs that you need to address? Invite God into this question, writing in the following space anything you sense God putting on your heart or mind. Share this list with your Bible study leader or an accountability partner so that she can work with you on important next steps.

What blessings could result from deeper roots in these areas?

Whenever we reach a new level in our faith, whether we've just become a Christian or we have experienced some other spiritual breakthrough, our emotional and spiritual temperature soars! Even in this Bible study, I hope that you're experiencing new spiritual breakthroughs each week. But how do we keep our roots growing? How do we continue to experience the life and vibrancy that comes from our faith in Christ?

Remember my pitiful rhododendron? I planted that rhododendron the summer we purchased our home. I had dreams of a giant, flowering bush that would be the beautiful focal point of my backyard. If you've seen a rhododendron bush before, you know that a fully grown bush blooms with hundreds of flowers. When I planted that bush, I had hopes and dreams of such magnificent blooms.

In reality, there was only one bloom—just one giant purple bloom. Furthermore, that rhododendron bush had only three branches. It seemed that I owned the Charlie Brown version of a rhododendron bush.

What happened? Why didn't that plant explode with blooms? I neglected it. After I planted the bush, the new homeowner excitement wore off and I busied myself with other things. I never planned to neglect the bush. Every now and then I'd go out and pour some water around it and flick off a few of the bugs that were eating holes in leaves. But I neglected that plant. I didn't take care of it and nurture it into what I dreamed that it could be.

Read Ephesians 3:17. According to this verse, what do you need to do so that your roots will grow deeper in Christ?

Where are the places where you need to trust God more in your life?

I have found that the best way to cultivate trust in God is to read and memorize Scripture. It not only nourishes our roots, but it's also like a Global Positioning System (GPS). Here's a fun fact about me: I get lost almost everywhere I go. My GPS has saved me tremendous frustration—when I use it right. Likewise, I have what I like to call my personal GPS—God Positioning Scriptures—that help me when I get off track or am overwhelmed and unsure what to do next.

I like the idea of GPS verses because I am subjected to so many messages every day about how I look or my worth as a person. Whenever I hear words that might demean, discourage, or defeat me, I ask myself: *Barb, what are your GPS verses?* Whenever I need strength or redirection, I pull GPS verses from my memory and allow God's powerful, unchanging, life-giving words to encourage and sustain my heart. Practice and repetition help make this act as automatic as the good posture I learned by walking with a book on my head all those years ago.

Here is a favorite GPS verse from Matthew 6:33-34:

"Seek the Kingdom of God above all else, and live righteously, and he will give you everything you need.
"So don't worry about tomorrow, for tomorrow will bring its own worries. Today's trouble is enough for today."

Your challenge is to discover your GPS or God Positioning Scriptures. You can have one or many—it's up to you. Pull out your Bible or use your electronic device to locate verses that remind you of how precious you are in God's sight. If the idea of locating verses overwhelms you, there are a lot of verses in this book that you can highlight and memorize. For those of you who are new to the exercise, follow these steps:

1. Locate from one to three GPS verses that make you feel uplifted, encouraged, and strengthened when you read them.
2. Write each one on an index card or a small piece of paper.
3. Post the verses in a location where you will see them often and memorize one verse per week until you've memorized all three verses.
4. Pray and ask God to bring those verses back to mind whenever someone (including you!) says anything about your identity or worth that contradicts with God's truth about you.

Write down a GPS verse here that you want to memorize:

What drew you to this verse?

If we believe that God is true, good, and beautiful, then we must believe what He says about us. If the Bible is the record of God's words, then when we memorize God's words, we benefit from the power that resides in those words. We are strengthened and encouraged. Most of all, we have the ability to reject any statement, allegation, or claim that contradicts what God says about us.

Every single one of us can have strong roots. You don't have to be wrecked by the words of others. Dig deep by holding tight to God's Word. You can be strong, and you can stand tall!

Live It Out

1. **What is one thing that God impressed upon your heart during today's study?**

2. **What do you sense God leading you to think or do differently as a result of what you've studied?**

Talk with God

Take your GPS verse and use it for your prayer today. Ask God to help you live out that verse today.

Day 3: God Don't Like Ugly

Beauty Mark

Forgiveness brings inner and outer beauty.

Beauty Regimen

My maternal grandmother used to say "God don't like ugly." This statement usually followed a less-than-pleasant phone call or encounter with a friend or another woman from church. What Grandma meant was that any woman becomes ugly when she displays unfriendly or rude behavior.

I'm going to take Grandma's saying one step further and state that there is one thing guaranteed to make or keep a woman ugly: unforgiveness.

How can unforgiveness make you ugly? Stand in front of the mirror and think about the last person who made you mad. Replay your conversation with him or her. Pay particular attention to how your face looks when you repeat your portion of the conversation. Notice how much your face contorts and your lips curl. Beautiful? Not.

When someone hurts our feelings or does something to us, our faces pucker and our bodies tense up. Our shoulders draw back and our fists clench. We lose the supple fluidity of our movements, our beautiful gracefulness.

Unforgiveness is ugly. And my friends, God don't like ugly.

So we need consider what it is about unforgiveness that makes us ugly and how we can deal with it. God may intend to use today's study to free you from an ugly place in your life or help you reconcile with a difficult person. My prayer is that you give God permission to work in this area in your life. Whatever pain or anger God asks you to give up will be replaced by an infusion of God-given beauty that will blossom within you and bring incalculable joy to your life.

Think about what you know about the character of God from the previous lessons. Is unforgiveness a part of God's character? Absolutely not! In fact, this behavior is the exact opposite of God's character, and anything that is contrary to God leads us away from God's best for us.

It might seem odd to include a lesson on unforgiveness in a study about beauty, but I suspect that for at least a few of you, God will use this lesson to do some much overdue business in your life.

A special note to those of you who may not have anyone in your life right now that you need to forgive: don't skip this part. Even if you aren't involved in a conflict right now, chances are you will need to forgive someone in the future.

Forgiveness is great—unless we're the ones who need to do the forgiving. Right now you are thinking about the person who has wronged you and thinking, "What? I'm not ready to set that person free! I hope that is not what you are about to ask me to do! You don't know what he or she has done to me. You better back off, Barb!"

When we're angry or hurt, forgiveness feels like trying to make butter with a toothpick. It just seems too hard. Though we hate the pain, we don't want to let go of it until justice is done.

It's important to clarify what forgiveness is *not*:

1. Forgiveness isn't forgetting about the offense.
2. Forgiveness isn't waiting for a certain period of time to pass. Time does not heal all wounds.
3. Forgiveness isn't saying, "God, you forgive them. But I'm not going to."
4. Most of all, forgiveness isn't forcing yourself to be in contact with a person who is still engaged in bad behavior and hasn't acknowledged it. You do not have to allow someone to continue to hurt you.

What do we want from those who have hurt us? That's easy. We want them to take responsibility for their actions and say things like "I'm sorry" and "I was wrong." Next, we want them to tell us how badly they feel about their mistake and to suffer as much as we have.

But what happens if they never step up? What do we do if they refuse to take responsibility for their misdeeds? What if those persons are dead or otherwise inaccessible? Does that mean our lives are permanently damaged as a result?

It doesn't have to be that way. We still can forgive. Forgiveness is setting someone free from a debt that is owed to you as a result of a wrong done against you.

Read Matthew 18:21-22 in the margin. What was Jesus' response to Peter's question?

Peter knew that forgiveness is necessary when we are offended, but he questioned the extent to which another deserves forgiveness. With his question, we see that Peter wondered whether or not there are limits on forgiveness. Jesus blew the lid off limits, casting a vision that our forgiveness should be modeled after God's unlimited forgiveness.

> *Forgiveness is setting someone free from a debt that is owed to you as a result of a wrong done against you.*

21 Then Peter came to him and asked, "Lord, how often should I forgive someone who sins against me? Seven times?" 22 "No, not seven times," Jesus replied, "but seventy times seven!" (Matthew 18:21-22)

What happens to us when we keep score on the people who hurt or offend us?

What are some of the ugly feelings associated with unforgiveness?

How does harboring unforgiveness impact our hearts, minds, and spiritual lives?

I believe that forgiveness can restore beauty. When we collect and catalog ugly words and memories, those painful narratives wear on our souls and our bodies. In my book *Enough Already*, I share a story about how my grandmother struggled with ulcers, a symptom of unforgiveness toward my grandfather, who had been unfaithful. At a certain point in my childhood, my grandmother made the decision to forgive. Her forgiveness actually changed our family. Furthermore, unforgiveness gave Grandma her beauty back. She radiated the love of Christ to so many in our community!

Beauty also can be restored when we embrace forgiveness for ourselves. How many of us have accepted God's forgiveness but are still hanging on to regrets from the past? The Scriptures tell us that if the Son has set us free, then we are free indeed (John 8:36)! Freedom through forgiveness is a gift that we delight in for ourselves and share with others.

Is there someone or a group of people from your beauty narrative that you need to forgive? What did they do or say that hurt you deeply?

Are there times when you struggle with forgiveness, especially when you have to forgive the same person multiple times?

In Luke 7 we read about a visit Jesus made to the home of a religious leader named Simon. A woman described as an immoral woman entered the home. The woman stopped in front of Jesus and knelt down. In today's society, that scene would have been described on Facebook or Twitter with updates that would have launched a thousand scandals.

Read Luke 7:36-50 and answer the following questions:

What did the woman do with the expensive perfume that she brought with her?

Why do you suppose that she sobbed as she anointed Jesus' feet with the perfume?

In verses 44-48, Jesus compares Simon's heart attitude to the woman's heart attitude. What did Jesus reveal about this woman's heart?

What were Jesus' final words to the woman in verse 50?

Imagine how it must have felt to be that immoral woman, now a forgiven woman. She stood up, free from the burden of sinful living, a woman who was deeply aware of how flawed and sinful she was. She was forgiven! Could you imagine the smile on her face and the light in her eyes? There's nothing more beautiful than the look of joy and freedom on someone's face. The tremendous burden of sin was lifted from her heart, and once it was removed, the God-given beauty within her shined through.

People are going to make mistakes. You are going to make mistakes. Someone that you know will say or do something that will cause you pain. That's a given. Would you want to live in a world where there are limits to the forgiveness that you can receive? If not, then should you place limits on the forgiveness that you are willing to extend to others?

Read Colossians 3:13a in the margin. What does it mean to make allowances for each other's faults? How can we do this?

> Make allowance for each other's faults, and forgive anyone who offends you. (Colossians 3:13a)

> *Our capacity to forgive is directly related to our understanding of how much we have been forgiven.*

Who are we instructed to forgive? Are there any exceptions?

Here's the lesson that we need to remember about forgiveness: our capacity to forgive is directly related to our understanding of how much we have been forgiven.

When we don't practice forgiveness, each offense becomes like a brick wall in the heart. Brick walls can be protective, but they also can be barriers. Some of you have built barriers in your hearts. You've been hurt so much by so many people that you've built brick walls twenty feet high.

It doesn't have to be that way. You *can* forgive.

How can you know when you've forgiven someone? Here are three clues:

1. You think of that person's name and don't rehearse the wound or wrong.
2. You don't get jealous or angry when others speak of that person.
3. You can pray for the person and ask God to bless him or her.

You can make the decision to forgive. It won't be an easy decision, but each time you think of the person who offended you, choose to speak the words "I forgive you" in that moment. Each time you speak those words, you chip away at the pain and anger. Each time you speak forgiveness, you tear down the bars that the prison of pain wants to build around you. Forgiveness opens your heart and allows your beauty to shine through.

Share a story of a time when you forgave someone who hurt you. How did you know that you had forgiven the person?

Before we close today's lesson, I'd like to say a few words about reconciliation. There is a huge difference between forgiveness and reconciliation. Misunderstanding the two can actually prevent someone from engaging in the forgiveness process. Let's review the definition of forgiveness and add to it a definition of reconciliation:

Forgiveness: Setting someone free from a debt that is owed to you as a result of a wrong done against you.

Reconciliation: The process through which broken relationships are restored.

There are conditions and rules for reconciliation. Don't misunderstand this: God desires reconciliation. We know this because the Bible tells us that God's desire is to reconcile the world to himself (see 2 Corinthians 5:19; Colossians 1:20). However, our human choices sometimes get in the way of reconciliation. Here are some of the conditions for reconciliation:

1. Reconciliation requires the willingness of all parties involved.
2. The bad behavior should have ended, and each party should have an assurance of safety.
3. There is to be a desire for all sides to come together.
4. Each party has to take responsibility for his or her behavior or actions.

There are some situations when reconciliation isn't going to be possible or wise. But there are other times when reconciliation doesn't work out because the other person just isn't ready yet.

Read Romans 12:18 in the margin. Even if the other party demonstrates bad behavior, what is our obligation?

> Do all that you can to live in peace with everyone. (Romans 12:18)

Forgiveness is beautiful! When we release our bitterness or pain from the past, it's an instant lift for our hearts, our minds, and even our faces. If this is a journey that you need to take, begin to memorize the verses from today's study and allow God to guide you toward forgiveness and, if the other person is willing, reconciliation. There's nothing too great for God to forgive, and best of all, God will give you the strength and the power to forgive too!

Live It Out

1. **What is one thing that God impressed upon your heart during today's study?**

2. **What do you sense God leading you to think or do differently as a result of what you've studied?**

Talk with God

Has today's study revealed any areas of unforgiveness? If so, are you ready to choose forgiveness with God's help? If the answer is yes, then go ahead and pray to God, acknowledging that you are making the decision to forgive whatever the situation is on your heart and mind and asking for God's supernatural help. Then consider whether or not reconciliation is possible and, if it is, begin to work toward it.

If you aren't ready to forgive, then tell God about your struggle. Ask God to soften your heart and help you choose to forgive just as He has forgiven you.

Day 4: Just Like Eyebrows, Two Are Better Than One

Beauty Mark
We need connections with other women.

Beauty Regimen

At its essence, friendship is connection. As humans, we long for connection. As women, we need connection. Guys need connection too, but we *need* connection! There are so many things swirling through our hearts and minds that we need the help of other women to sort through—so many ups and downs in life that we need female connections in order to get through.

Yet I know that many women struggle with friendships with other women. We know that we should be friends, but there is a lot of fear and mistrust that gets in the way. Here's one Christian woman's response:

I don't have a bestie—a good friend, maybe. "Frenenemies" at work at best. I am in small groups but don't really feel I belong.

There is a difference between knowing lots of people and being connected. Connection happens when we allow ourselves to be known and we get to know others. Some of you avoid this connection out of fear; others just don't think you need a close connection.

Belonging is essential, but it shouldn't be exclusive. Our lives shouldn't be about looking for that perfect "bestie" and endangering current relationships in the process. Sometimes we overanalyze our relationships with one another, don't we?

When's the last time I talked to so-and-so?
Do I need to call her?
Why isn't she calling me?
Is she mad at me?
Why did she say that on Facebook?
Should I apologize?
Why isn't she calling me to apologize?

It's no wonder we can tire of the drama of being friends with other women!

What do friendship and connection have to do with our ugly struggle with beauty? We need the support of friendship and connection as we battle our ugly struggle with beauty. And once we finally believe that we are beautiful because God created us, we need to have supportive, godly women in our lives to encourage and remind us of that truth!

During my undergraduate years at Bowling Green State University, one of the constant rules for women on campus was "never walk alone in the dark." Now, a woman could physically walk from one place on campus to another in the dark, but university staff and police strongly discouraged it. Why? Because in the dark, there were unforeseen dangers that a woman, even a strong woman, might not be able to fight off alone.

When it comes to our ugly struggle with beauty, we can be victorious, but we'll always need to maintain our victory. There are times when insecurity, a battle with cancer, or the collapse of a relationship might temporarily shake us up like an earthquake. However, the amount of residual damage will be lessened if we recognize this principle: *there is safety and victory in numbers.*

Read Exodus 17:8-13. What did Aaron and Hur do for Moses that he couldn't do on his own?

If Moses had been stubborn or prideful and turned away their help, what would have happened to the Israelites as a result?

At a conference, I listened to author and organizational physiologist Adam Grant talk about three kinds of people: givers, takers, and matchers.

1. Givers enjoy helping others with no strings attached.
2. Takers engage in interactions in order to get things.
3. Matchers like to keep things balanced and operate by quid pro quo.

I'm divided equally between being a giver and a matcher. The thought of being seen as a taker could melt me right on the spot. But, as Grant pointed out, all three types of people have a function and role. When it comes to takers, Grant says that many of them used to be givers or matchers but got burned somewhere along the way. Givers and matchers seem like the best options, but they can be taken advantage of in a situation and become bitter.

How easy or difficult is it for you to accept help or advice from a friend?

__ very easy   __ somewhat easy
__ somewhat difficult   __ very difficult

What are some of the hesitations or fears that prevent you from freely accepting help?

When it comes to your friendships with other women, do you tend to be more of a giver, taker, or matcher?

During my growing up years, I longed for another girl who would consider me to be her best friend. I had lots of friends, but in my teenage view, the epitome of belonging was the "best friend" status. I wanted to know that I would be someone's first phone call to make plans on a Friday night. I wanted to be the first person she shared a joke with at lunchtime or the one she chose to link arms with while walking down the hallway. As I reflect on my teenage self, I try to be kind to the memory of that tall, outwardly confident but insecure girl. She wanted to be loved and valued as someone's best friend.

We all want to be liked by others. Often our internal friendship monitor keeps tabs on what other people are doing but not always on how we operate in friendships. It's easy for us to live by the "what have you done for me lately?" mind-set.

Instead, let's look at what the Bible says about the qualities we should be adding to our relationships.

Read Colossians 3:12 in the margin. Paul uses clothing as a metaphor for the qualities that we should carry with us into our relationships with others. What are those qualities?

Circle the qualities that are most difficult for you. Explain why in the space below:

Are there any relationships or friendships in your life that would be transformed if you increased any of the qualities you circled? If so, how would they be transformed?

Did you know that a porcupine has around thirty thousand quills on its body? These sharp, pointy quills protect the creature from other animals or humans that might want to hurt it. However, those same quills also get in the way of allowing the porcupine to get close to other porcupines for warmth.

When harsh weather conditions strike, porcupines gather together in clusters to find protection from the elements. If the porcupines rushed toward each other with their quills up, it would create mass injury—and likely a lot of fights. Yet a lone porcupine in harsh conditions won't survive. So what's a porcupine to do?

In order for porcupines to get close to each other, they have to lower their quills close to their skin. Only then are they able to gather close together.

Sometimes we can be hurt by other women. Perhaps someone gossiped about you or pretended to be your friend, but her actions and behavior inflicted wounds on your heart and soul. Other "quills" such as envy, lies, anger, or hatred get under our skin and rile us up! When this happens, it's tempting to cut ourselves off from making or cultivating friendships with

> Since God chose you to be the holy people he loves, you must clothe yourselves with tenderhearted mercy, kindness, humility, gentleness, and patience. (Colossians 3:12)

Extra Insight:

Before speaking,
ask yourself:

T – Is it True?
H – Is it Helpful?
I – Is it Inspiring?
N – Is it Necessary?
K – Is it Kind?

other women in order to protect ourselves. (In this case, I'm not talking about women who have displayed dangerous behaviors toward you.)

Yet like the porcupine, we cannot survive alone. In fact, we were not designed to be alone. The beauty of our female heart is that it was created to love, share, nurture, and bless other women, who have lives just as complicated as our own.

Imagine that you are a porcupine. You have thirty thousand quills on your body, and you can choose to keep them up or put them down.

When are you more likely to put up your "quills" in conversations or interactions with other women?

Read Romans 12:18 in the margin. According to this verse, what is your responsibility?

One of the essential elements of friendship is love. There are many ways to express love, but Scripture outlines a kind of love that reflects God's character.

Read 1 Corinthians 13:4-7 below, and write your name above every instance of the words *love* and *it*.

Love is patient and kind. Love is not jealous or boastful

or proud or rude. It does not demand its own way. It is

not irritable, and it keeps no record of being wronged.

It does not rejoice about injustice but rejoices whenever

the truth wins out. Love never gives up, never loses

faith, is always hopeful, and endures through every

circumstance.

Now underline the phrases describing how you want to increase your level of love in friendships.

Are there any practical actions that came to mind as you did this exercise?

Live It Out

1. What is one thing that God impressed upon your heart during today's study?

2. What do you sense God leading you to think or do differently as a result of what you've studied?

Talk with God

Who do you need to pray for today? Which one of your friends would appreciate your prayers right now? Lift her up in prayer and then give her a call to find out if there are some practical ways you can show her God's love.

Day 5: Three Different Types of Friendships

Beauty Mark
God uses different kinds of friendships to enrich our lives.

Beauty Regimen

Throughout the Bible we read about the different types of community and relationships that people have with one another. As women, we need different kinds of community in our lives because God ministers to us through different interpersonal dynamics. Today we're going to look at three different kinds of relationships that support us in winning our ugly struggle with beauty:

1. Spiritual Friendships
2. Mentor-Mentee Relationships
3. "Go-to" Girls

Today, we're going to look at examples of each of these relationships in Scripture as well as practical tips on how to integrate these needed relationships into your life.

1. Spiritual Friendships

This is the kind of group where Jesus makes the difference! When women gather, the topic of conversation can cover an expanse as wide as the Atlantic. However, the goal of spiritual friendships is to connect and challenge one another to ongoing discipleship in Christ. Connection creates the opportunity for women to get to know one another and share in one another's lives. Then a challenge takes place when women agree to be accountable to others in the group. Challenge doesn't mean confrontation or competition. Rather, it's about honesty and the permission to provide loving feedback.

Spiritual friendships bond like superglue. As women talk each week about where God is moving in their lives and hear how other women are stepping up to follow God's leadings in bold ways, everyone's faith grows along with their connection to one another.

Spiritual friendship groups flow along with the lives of the women present. Free-flowing conversation is what drives this group—versus more structured Bible study. I've had long-term spiritual friendship groups, and our life circumstances became the backdrop for spiritual discussion and challenge.

We see spiritual friendships modeled in Scripture. After Jesus ascended to heaven, the apostles continued to preach in Jesus' name. As the gospel message took root in the hearts of people, the number of believers grew, and some wonderful things happened as a result of those new relationships.

Read Ecclesiastes 4:9-12 in the margin. What is the danger of solitude? What are the blessings that come from partnering with others?

A spiritual friendship group should have three or four women. This kind of group often begins organically, meaning that there's no sign-up sheet or structured Bible study. In my experience, spiritual friendship group attendees are often Bible study or small-group leaders but enjoy having a place where they can talk about their faith without a structured study format.

What should you talk about at a spiritual friendship gathering? The format is simple! Here are the questions that you can ask during each week's meeting:

1. What are you celebrating in your life? Where are you struggling?
2. Where do you see God working in your life these days?
3. What are you praying about?
4. What have you read in the Bible lately that is challenging you to think or behave differently?
5. Who are you praying for and serving?
6. As you've listened to the other women share about their lives, how do you think God might be leading you to think or act differently?

While this isn't a structured Bible study group, it would be expected that someone will pull out a Bible or access an online Bible app to share a verse or insight. It's always a good idea to have someone be the "heart" of the group, making sure that each woman has the chance to share or to discern whether or not deeper needs exist.

2. Mentor-Mentee Relationships

Mentoring happens when one person opens herself (or himself) up so that another may learn and grow. One of the misconceptions is that a person must have vast knowledge and resources before agreeing to mentor another. If a mentor's key role is to train or advise, then a mentor really only needs to be farther ahead of the person looking for guidance or instruction.

While the Bible never uses the word *mentor*, there are several examples in the Bible of mentoring relationships. A few examples include Moses and Joshua, Elijah and Elisha, Elizabeth and Mary, and Paul and Timothy.

As leader of the Israelites, Moses was responsible for shepherding God's people through their wilderness journey. Moses was often assisted by a young man named Joshua. As the Israelites traveled and fought off enemies, Joshua had the opportunity to talk to and learn from a great leader. Moses took the time to train Joshua and then activate those emerging skills.

Yesterday we read about Aaron and Hur in Exodus 17:8-13. Review these verses again, focusing this time on Joshua's role. What did Moses ask Joshua to do? What was the outcome?

While we can't be 100 percent certain, chances are that Moses did not have special weekly training classes for Joshua. They would have talked regularly as the Israelites traveled from one location to the next. Moses would have coached Joshua before and after different assignments.

If you are familiar with Joshua's story, he took on many great challenges and showed great faithfulness to God throughout his life. In fact, God told Moses to commission Joshua as the next leader of the Israelites. As Moses' life on earth neared the end, he imparted some powerful final words to Joshua.

Read Deuteronomy 31:7. What did Moses call Joshua to do?

Looking at the experiences of Moses and Joshua and other biblical mentoring relationships, we might be intimidated by the idea of mentoring. As I've mentioned, sometimes we think that in order to be a mentor, we must have all of the answers; and we're afraid to admit that we don't. And if we're on the other side of the relationship, it can be embarrassing for us to admit how much we don't know about our faith.

What exactly does a mentoring relationship look like? Here's a framework that I use in my mentoring relationships:

1. New mentoring relationships should last from six months to two years.
2. Mentor and mentee should meet at least twice a month. It is up to the mentee to contact the mentor for scheduling and confirm the appointment. (Why? Mentors usually have very busy schedules, and the mentees can demonstrate their commitment by doing the follow-up to confirm the appointment.)
3. Suggested curriculum or course of study can vary based on the area that the mentee needs to work on. As always, Scripture is a great resource for mentoring.

4. The meeting should last one to one and a half hours. For courtesy's sake, every effort should be made to start and end on time.

5. Important: For the initial meeting, mentor and mentee should just try to get to know each other and determine whether appropriate chemistry or commitment exists. If not, this should be addressed immediately, and the search for a new mentor should begin.

6. The win of a mentor-mentee relationship is that both individuals feel spiritually encouraged and challenged. The person who is being mentored gets time, wisdom, and encouragement from someone who has "been there done that." Mentors benefit from the challenge of nurturing someone in her faith.

My last mentoring relationship lasted two years. I met with this talented young woman regularly, and we would talk about her spiritual, emotional, relational, and professional life. During those two years, I watched her develop and grow—even through a life-changing challenge that she encountered. When our regular meeting times ended, we were no longer mentor-mentee but close friends. Although mentoring relationships don't always end that way, you should be able to recognize that God showed up and transformed each of you.

3. "Go-to" Girls

When tragedy strikes, you've got to have a "go-to girl." This is the friend who knows all your secrets and can handle all your stuff. Your "go-to girl" doesn't have all the answers for your drama, but she's always there for you in a crisis; and you can trust her no matter what.

It was 6:00 A.M. on Sunday morning when my cell phone rang. I'm usually not up that early on Sunday, but I had to get to church early that day to prepare for the morning's activities, so I awoke thirty minutes earlier than usual. I snatched up my phone to view the caller ID. It was one of my closest girlfriends. I answered, "Hello."

Sobs. All I could hear were soft, steady sobs. In that moment I knew that no one had died but something had died in her heart. I took a deep breath and simply said, "I'm here."

We sat in silence for several moments. As one who has sobbed on the other end, there's nothing more soothing than knowing that the other person is willing to just sit and wait, unrushed until words are ready to come.

After a few moments, she began to talk. Out poured a story of late night events that overflowed into the early morning hours—her painful recollections broke and joined my heart to hers simultaneously. I wanted to drop my flatiron and rush over to her house, but that wasn't an option. She just needed me to be her friend and be present in her pain. We prayed together that morning and for many days after that. As sad as that event was, I was grateful that she had invited me to share that difficult space in her life.

That friend is one of my "go-to girls." This is what I call a select group of four women in my life whom I call—or who call me—when life turns upside down. Ladies, you've got to have at least one "go-to girl" in your life. (By the way, notice how I said "go-to girl," not "go-to guy"? There are lots of reasons why this kind of friendship should only be with another woman.)

In the Bible, there's a wonderful story about a woman named Ruth and her decision to be a "go-to girl" for her mother-in-law, Naomi. After the death of her husband, Ruth was faced with a choice: to stay with her widowed mother-in-law or return to her homeland.

Read Ruth 1:16-18. What did Ruth declare to Naomi?

Like Ruth and Naomi, "Go-to girls" are there for each other no matter what! These friendships are characterized by vulnerability, transparency, and high levels of trust. No flakiness allowed! This means that "go-to girl" relationships are scary at the beginning because trust must be built over time.

Do you have any current and active "go-to girl" relationships?

__ yes   __ no   __ I'm working on it

If you need to develop some of those relationships, here are a few tips to remember:

1. A prospective "go-to girl" is already in your life. Think about those women with whom you have some chemistry and some level of trust.
2. Ask each of these women out to coffee or lunch once or twice a month. Talk about your life and ask her questions about her life. Keep the conversation light.
3. As you connect with certain women regularly on a one-on-one basis, conversation should steer toward deeper life issues. Continue to assess whether or not the level of vulnerability or transparency feels mutual.
4. Invite a friend to "come along" on a bad day! Our close friends want us to reach out, so do it! What's the point of having "go-to girls" if you're going to keep to yourself?

If you've never experienced any of these three types of relationships, relax. You don't have to figure everything out at once. Begin by observing your existing relationships with women, and then pray. Ask God to give you opportunities to move deeper into these kinds of relationships over coffee or lunch. In time, you should be able to determine whether a woman in your life could be a spiritual friend, a mentor or mentee, or a "go-to-girl." You might have to explain to some what these kinds of relationships involve, but don't let that stop you from committing yourself to developing these needed relationships in your life.

Live It Out

1. What is one thing that God impressed upon your heart during today's study?

2. What do you sense God leading you to think or do differently as a result of what you've studied?

Talk with God

Creating new relationships can be intimidating, especially friendships like the ones we've studied today. God loves community. If this is an area where you struggle, ask God for opportunities to practice developing these kinds of relationships.

GENTLE AND QUIET BEAUTY

Don't be concerned about the outward beauty of fancy hairstyles, expensive jewelry, or beautiful clothes. You should clothe yourselves instead with the beauty that comes from within, the unfading beauty of a _____ and _____ spirit, which is so precious to God.

(1 Peter 3:3-4)

Gentleness – _____ attitude, _____ behavior, _____ character

Quietness – choosing to possess _____, deep _____, _____

But the Holy Spirit produces this kind of fruit in our lives: love, joy, peace, patience, kindness, goodness, faithfulness, gentleness, and self-control. (Galatians 5:22-23a)

1 Samuel 25:23-25 – Abigail spoke the truth to David in a humble and respectful way.

A _____ _____ deflects anger,
*   but harsh words make tempers flare.*
*   (Proverbs 15:1)*

A beautiful woman who lacks _____
*   is like a gold ring in a pig's snout.*
*   (Proverbs 11:22)*

Reacting with a gentle and quiet spirit is not always easy to do, but it is the most _____ thing that we can do if we want to have the _____ that allows God to use us.

We must let the Holy Spirit redecorate our hearts.

God wants us to be beautiful inside out, but _____ can cloud the ability of others to see God's beauty in us.

Then she knelt behind him at his feet, weeping. Her tears fell on his feet, and she wiped them off with her hair. Then she kept kissing his feet and putting perfume on them. (Luke 7:38)

"I tell you, her sins—and they are many—have been forgiven, so she has shown me much love. But a person who is forgiven little shows only little love." Then Jesus said to the woman, "Your sins are forgiven." (Luke 7:47-48)

When we recognize how much we have been _____ through

what Jesus Christ did for us on the cross, then what response do we have but to

_____others.

Week 5

WINNING OUR UGLY STRUGGLE

Memory Verse

"Your faith has saved you; go in peace." (Luke 7:50)

This Week's Theme

Inner beauty flows out of us toward others when we experience Jesus' peace and healing.

What it means to be a woman is profound. How God has crafted the feminine body on the inside and out blows our understanding and imaginations. Think about how your mom's body accommodated your growth and development, not to mention how God created her body to evict you at a certain date in time. I love being a woman because I appreciate God's workmanship and am impressed with the body He created for me, even though there are times when being a woman is hard and painful.

Let's be honest: there are some things about being a woman that are difficult, embarrassing, or downright uncomfortable to talk about with others—things that happen within us and things that happen to us. For a long time I struggled to find a comfortable way to engage in conversation about women's issues. Once upon a time, I was a tomboy. After I outgrew Barbies, I loved playing kickball and regularly wore out the knees in my jeans through rough-and-tumble play. Mom, bless her heart, wanted to prepare me for the changes that I'd go through, but the topic of female development made me anxious and very, very uncomfortable.

I want to acknowledge that talking about certain topics—from menstruation to the wounds we receive because of our identities as women—can be uncomfortable for some of us. Even as we recognize that God designed our bodies, including their various functions, we may be uneasy about some topics—particularly as they relate to areas where we have been hurt and are in need of healing. So why would I introduce sensitive topics related to our femininity within the broader discussion of inner beauty? There are a few reasons:

1. We are created by and in the image of a holy God, so every part of our bodies has the stamp of God's goodness on it.
2. The Bible often uses the female body as a metaphor when talking about different spiritual topics.
3. Ultra-sensitive subjects such as menstrual cycles actually get a fair amount of attention in Scripture, so it would be an oversight not to address this topic since we are discussing the beauty and wholeness of our feminine bodies, inside and out.

So this week we will touch upon the uniquely feminine aspects of our bodies as we explore how we become fragmented and broken inside when we allow others, rather than Christ, to define our identities. We will consider some common ways we as women can be wounded and broken—especially related to our identities as women and our sexuality. And we will find hope and healing as we invite the peace of Christ to restore us, creating an inner beauty that radiates outward.

Day 1: Internal Brokenness and Fragmentation

Beauty Mark

Knowing our identities in Christ keeps us from confusion.

Beauty Regimen

When we study Scripture, we can see that Eve was always in God's plans.

In Genesis 2, God placed Adam in the garden of Eden but remarked that Adam's solitary state needed to change. However, God didn't immediately create Eve; rather, God gave Adam the task of naming all of the animals first.

God brought the animals to Adam. After awhile, Adam would have noticed that the animals were created with distinctive features that we'd refer to as male and female parts. How long do you think it took Adam to realize that he didn't have a partner or counterpart?

After naming all of the animals, Adam fell into a God-induced sleep. And here's my favorite part: Adam exclaimed, "At last!" when he saw Eve (Genesis 2:23). Not only had the longing for companionship been satisfied, but Adam realized Eve to be complementary yet distinct. Their bodies were different, but those two bodies were designed to fit together as one as husband and wife. While it might seem that creating Eve occurred to God as an afterthought, God had planned for Eve all along.

Imagine the hand of God shaping the delicate curve of her neck or smoothing her many contours. Upon the first look, Adam would have immediately noticed the differences between himself and Eve.

Here's a question to think about: what if God had created Adam and Eve with different exteriors but made them exactly the same on the inside (so that they could not be joined together as one)? How would that have changed their ability to connect with each other? What would be forever lost from the richness of that distinct physical relationship and union designed for husband and wife? God planned for men and women to be internally and externally distinct.

Furthermore, who we are as women—regardless of our marital status—impacts our world deeply and uniquely every day. Consider single women such as Susan B. Anthony, Coco Chanel, Mother Teresa, Condoleezza Rice, and Tyra Banks. The gifts and talents of these women span the spectrum of society and culture, and each one has made her mark in a distinctly feminine way.

Today we're going to talk about our identities as beautifully and uniquely created women and why the Bible calls us to be integrated on the inside and out. Let's get started with a question.

Answer this question: Who am I?

How do you know who you are? What anchors your understanding of yourself?

If you are a Christian, the answer should be Christ. Our identity as Christ-followers can be captured in the following statements:

"I am a child of God." (John 1:12)
"I am a new creation." (2 Corinthians 5:17)
"I am forgiven." (Ephesians 1:17)
"I am alive in Christ." (Ephesians 2:5)

These are just a few identity descriptions that we can use to answer the question "Who am I?" Yet many of us struggle to answer that question.

"I don't know who I am. I don't know what I stand for." These are the words of eighteen-year-old model and social media sensation Essena O'Neill. In November 2015, she shocked Instagram and YouTube viewers by announcing that she was quitting social media. With hundreds of thousands of followers and eager advertisers, O'Neill raked in substantial income posting photos and videos of herself. One day she realized that she didn't know who she was, and her identity crisis frightened her into making a life-altering decision. In her final YouTube video, which she dedicated to her twelve-year-old self, O'Neill explained why she quit social media. She admitted that she had become addicted to social media and social approval, and that even though she had it all, she was miserable. She said, "When you let yourself be defined by numbers, you let yourself be defined by something that is not real, that is not pure, and that is not love."[1]

The truth is, we can all experience an identity crisis—no matter our age or stage in life. You might have felt amazing at one time but later found yourself floundering. Perhaps a relationship ended and you weren't sure who you were by yourself. Maybe your career supported your identity, and when that job was gone you were left wondering what your life should be about.

Extra Insight:

We all have times when we feel unsure about who we are or what we should be doing. The most important thing to do during uncertain times is to link back to what we know to be true.

Read 2 Corinthians 1:22 in the margin. What does the Apostle Paul say about the identity of those who've placed their faith in Jesus Christ?

If our identity is in Christ, then what does that mean for how we are to think and live?

In his Letter to the Galatians, Paul addresses the identity issue again, specifically for himself. Look up Galatians 2:20. How does Paul define his identity?

Now let's merge 2 Corinthians 1:22 and Galatians 2:20. If Christ lives within you as your identity, then...

1. **What is the purpose of your life?**

2. **How will you set your decision-making compass for all areas of your life?**

3. **When you are confused about your personal liberties or boundaries, whose standard will you rely upon?**

While we as Christians understand that our identity is in Christ, we live in a society that doesn't share that belief; and there is confusion about what to believe regarding who we are as men and women. Jesus' willingness to come to earth as a man affirms the importance of our bodies and the integrated nature of our hearts, souls, minds, and bodies.

Read Mark 12:30 in the margin. How are we called to love God?

"And you must love the LORD your God with all your heart, all your soul, all your mind, and all your strength."
(Mark 12:30)

Earlier in this study, we learned about how we are created in the image of God. There is a wholeness to God that is stamped upon our human bodies, and that stamp remains even though we are marred by sin. Our devotion to God comes from a place of wholeness. We bring all that we are to God and offer all of it.

The danger of not knowing our identities in Christ is that we become fragmented in our emotions, thoughts, and behaviors without anything to unify us within ourselves. Such internal brokenness is profoundly painful. When we're fragmented, our fragmented choices lead to frustrating and fearful consequences.

Live It Out

1. What is one thing that God impressed upon your heart during today's study?

2. What do you sense God leading you to think or do differently as a result of what you've studied?

Talk with God

At the end of today's study, there are two landing pads: standing firm in your identity in Christ or allowing others to determine your identity. If you are struggling to overcome things that have been said or done to you as a woman, then bring those to God and ask Him to lead you and guide you through that struggle.

Extra Insight:

"You're not defined by your feelings. You're not defined by the opinions of others or by your circumstances. You're not defined by your successes or failures. You're not defined by the car you drive, the money you make, or the house you say you own when the bank really does. You are defined by God and God alone. He identifies you as his own."
—Rick Warren[3]

Day 2: Healing from the Inside Out

Beauty Mark
When we cry out to Jesus, He gives us peace.

Beauty Regimen

One summer day, my mother called a few of my female cousins and me into the house to talk. We were all about nine or ten years old at the time. As we settled onto the edge of my mom's bed, she pulled a little booklet out of a very large box with "Stayfree" written on top. Then she began to read to us about three young girls learning about the "wonderful changes" in their blossoming bodies. There was nothing wonderful about what my mother was reading to us. Frankly, I was horrified. And I had questions:

"You mean that I am going to bleed for almost seven days?"
"Yes."
"And this is going to happen *each month*?"
"Yes."
"Every single month?"
"Except for when you are pregnant and going to have a baby."
"*This* is where babies come from?"

I wanted to crawl into a hole right then and there. As my mother shared information that both intrigued and horrified me at the same time, I was burdened with new knowledge about a part of myself I couldn't see and didn't completely understand. Yet I sensed a tremendous holiness about the topic.

For some of you, monthly menstrual cycles are a thing of the past. Whether through menopause or medical intervention, you have been freed from this part of our female experience. And I can hear you whispering "hallelujah" under your breath. But you've got daughters, sisters, and friends who are still navigating this monthly odyssey.

Beautiful isn't the word we associate with our periods; we use words like *painful, inconvenient, embarrassing,* even *debilitating.* Even though modern innovations such as maxi pads, tampons, cups, and injections have worked to minimize the inconvenience of our menstrual cycles, many of us still feel that we are suffering each month.

Yet we have so much to be thankful for! Did you know that in ancient Greece women wrapped lint around small pieces of wood for tampons, and in ancient Rome, women made tampons and pads of soft wool? When the commercial sanitary pad came to market in 1896, the product failed because women weren't willing to be seen in the store purchasing them.[4]

Unless pregnant or ill, every menstruating woman has a cycle that shows up once a month. The average woman menstruates every twenty-eight days for approximately forty years. This translates to 3,500 days or 450 weeks of her life.

In Mark 5, we read about a woman who had been constantly bleeding for twelve years. That's 4,380 days, which is 880 more days than the average woman over a lifetime! Take a moment and let that sink into your mind. She approached Jesus and the disciples as they traveled to the home of a religious leader whose daughter had just died.

Read Mark 5:24-26. What do you learn about the woman and her condition?

Could you imagine what it would be like to suffer as she had for so many years? Her condition impacted every aspect of her life:

- Under the religious laws of the time, menstruating women were considered unclean, so she would have been separated from her household and community. Most women endured this for the normal seven days, but after a few years, this woman probably lost her husband and family because she wouldn't have been permitted to fulfill her role as a wife and mother.
- Some translations use the word *hemorrhage* when describing the issue of blood. It's possible that her flow was so heavy she may have soaked through her ancient menstrual padding hourly.
- The doctors of the time likely would have subjected her to experimental treatments to try to eliminate the flow; and knowing how desperate she was, those doctors probably would have charged a large sum.
- Due to the substantial loss of blood, the woman likely had anemia. This meant she would have been weak, frail, and vulnerable during all of those years.

Is there something you've been suffering through for many years that has been draining your joy and energy for life? Describe the situation and the impact on your life:

Then there was the day when the woman saw Jesus walking along the road. She didn't know all about Jesus that we know. We know about Jesus' faithfulness and the sacrifice He made so that we can have a relationship with Him. This woman didn't know those things. She only knew what people were saying about him. She had heard that Jesus raised people from the dead and healed people from their diseases. No doubt she wondered if Jesus could help her.

Ladies, none of us escapes this life without wounds. Some of us have been hurt so deeply that we feel as if we are hemorrhaging our lifeblood, with no end in sight. Like that woman, some of you may be drained from the circumstances of your life. Day after day, you drag yourself out of bed. You manage to survive the day just so that you can collapse back on your bed at night. Drawing your knees up to your chest, you weep. You cry out morning after morning for God to stop the bleeding, and at the end of each day you repeat that prayer again.

Read Mark 5:27-29. Why did the woman approach Jesus?

What happened as soon as she touched His robe?

The Scriptures tells us that in that moment her bleeding stopped and she knew that she was free from suffering. I wonder if her body tingled, or maybe she experienced a jolt. All we know is that she was healed from the inside out. Not only was her physical body healed, but that healing opened up other opportunities. The woman could now dream of rejoining her family and community.

When you are suffering on the inside, you don't want to think about beauty. You can't even see beauty because ugly feels like it is killing you. Even if the situation isn't your fault, you still suffer from painful memories and the fact that you can't find healing, no matter how hard you try.

I don't know what situation, circumstance, or life event feels like it is draining the life from you, but I do know this: You must reach out to Jesus. And you can't let anything stop you.

Read Hebrews 4:15-16 in the margin. What happens when we reach out to Jesus?

15 This High Priest of ours understands our weaknesses, for he faced all of the same testings we do, yet he did not sin. 16 So let us come boldly to the throne of our gracious God. There we will receive his mercy, and we will find grace to help us when we need it most. (Hebrews 4:15-16)

Is there something you need to stop and pray about right now? A situation that you've been suffering through for far too long? Take a moment to pray the prayer below or offer your own prayer.

Dear Jesus, I am drained from life. I am hemorrhaging from the pain of _____, and I don't know if I can make it another day. Jesus, I am coming to you like the hemorrhaging woman. I'm reaching out for you. I need the peace that you promised. Bless me with shalom. Bless me with wholeness and well-being. Give me peace. Amen.

In Mark 5:30, Jesus senses something has changed. Why?

This is quite an interesting verse, because the story mentions several times that there was a crowd pressing in on Jesus that day. Bodies jostled against one another to gain proximity to Christ. Desperate people were trying to get Jesus' attention, yet as soon as the woman touched Jesus, he noticed.

Now read Mark 5:31-34. What did the woman do? Why do you think her elation over healing turned to fear when she approached Jesus?

Under Jewish law, Jesus could have chastised her for touching Him while she was unclean. Instead, He gave her an opportunity to testify to what just happened in her life. The woman came to Jesus, fell to her knees, and told Him what happened.

I don't know about you, but I would have been a babbling mess in that moment. Not only would she have been terrified that she had offended Jesus but also she probably wondered how she could find the right words to express her thanks and gratitude.

Reread Mark 5:34. Why did Jesus say that the woman was healed?

When Jesus spoke again, His first word was *Daughter*. That tells us all we need to know about how Jesus felt about the woman. Jesus only used terms like sons and daughters when referring to believers.

Jesus' next statement to the woman is very powerful: "Go in peace." The word for "peace" is shalom. In this context, shalom speaks of wholeness, well-being, prosperity, security, friendship, and salvation entering into her life.

Peace is a beautiful thing, isn't it? Peace is living free from strife or worry. Peace is an inward calm that flows out through our facial expression, attitude, and behavior. Even when our solutions seem limited or our circumstances seem hopeless, peace can get us through to the other side.

Live It Out

1. **What is one thing that God impressed upon your heart during today's study?**

2. **What do you sense God leading you to think or do differently as a result of what you've studied?**

Talk with God

Did you identify something you need to pray about today? Is there a place in your life where you've been "bleeding out" for years, and now you realize that you need to cry out to Jesus? I don't know what your day holds, but I encourage you to be like the woman who didn't let anything stop her from reaching out to Jesus. Reach out to Jesus today. Seek Him in prayer now.

Day 3: What Scars Are For

Beauty Mark

Our scars tell a story of pain, healing, and God's faithfulness.

Beauty Regimen

I fell out of a tree when I was nine years old. Luckily, I was only about ten feet in the air and my hands slid down the trunk as I tumbled to the ground. Unfortunately, there was a small piece of metal at the base of the tree, and I cut my knee open on it. I don't remember if it hurt or not, but I do remember seeing a large, bloody gash and some white stuff coming out of the wound.

Like most kids, I ran into the house screaming my head off. My mom wasn't home, but Dad was there. My dad has always been a levelheaded guy, so the sight of a bunch of blood didn't faze him much. Neither did my gaping wound. In fact, Dad picked me up, set me on the bathroom vanity, and calmly poured peroxide over the wound. Then he gently pushed the white stuff back into the opening and slapped a bandage over the wound. When I asked him about the white stuff sticking out of my knee, he told me not to worry about it and sent me back outside to play.

Then Mom came home. She removed the bandage on my knee and glared at my dad; and they both drove me to the emergency room. Eight stitches and one painful tetanus shot later, I returned home with a huge wrap on my knee. After a round of antibiotics for an infection, my knee eventually healed. However, a large scar remained. I still have that scar today as a reminder of what I went through all those years ago.

When God created our bodies, He designed them with the capacity to heal and return to health under certain conditions. However, the healing process always includes a reminder, or scar, of what we've been through.

The scars on our bodies tell many stories. Depending on what we've been through, we proudly show some scars while hiding others. In any event, our scars are a constant, bittersweet reminder of certain life experiences that will never be erased from our memories or our bodies.

Not all wounds heal well. If an individual neglects to keep the injury site clean or constantly disrupts the injury, then a wound can heal poorly. Certain wounds can form scars, like keloids, that heal angry and red.[5] In certain cases, plastic surgeons are able to "revise" certain scars that have healed poorly. A skilled surgeon can use a variety of procedures to improve the cosmetic appearance, but that scar can never be completely replaced.[6]

Where are some of your physical scars located? What are some of the stories behind your scars?

When we consider the pain and difficulties that we face in this world, scars are a bittersweet yet appropriate metaphor for how God takes the horrible, painful events of our lives and redeems them. This is a fitting discussion because as we triumph in our ugly struggle with beauty, we've got to know how to live on the other side of that struggle. What do we do with the "scars" or reminders of both the physical and emotional wounds we've suffered during the heat of the battle?

Let's immerse ourselves in God's words of healing and redemption and see how Jesus' scars became the greatest redemptive symbol of all.

Prior to His crucifixion, Jesus was nailed to a cross. This meant that large spikes were nailed through his hands. While there are theologians and historians who debate the Greek words for wrists versus hands, no one debates the fact that a six- to eight-inch spike would do irreversible damage to Jesus' hands and feet. Not only were Jesus' hands and feet injured, but His side was punctured as well.

We can't begin to imagine the horror of Jesus' torture and death,[7] yet God raised Jesus from the dead. Not only that, Jesus appeared to small groups and then larger groups of people as proof of His resurrection.

Read Luke 24:35-40. When Jesus first appeared, why were the disciples frightened?

Why did Jesus tell them to look at His hands and feet (v. 39)?

When Jesus appeared to the group, it must have been quite a shock. When they last saw Jesus, he hung tortured on a cross before dying a painful death. Yet now he appeared before them with a living, whole body. He didn't look like the broken and bloody man they'd seen three days before. He stood before them with a resurrected body and healed wounds that bore a powerful reminder of his sacrifice for us.

What do Jesus' scars mean for us?

Before Jesus went to the cross, the soldiers who beat Jesus aimed to shame Him during the torture process as well. In Matthew 27, we read how the soldiers put a robe over Jesus' shredded back after He had been lashed with a whip. Then they shoved a crown of thorns on His head, pressing those sharp pricks down into His skin until blood flowed. Those soldiers mocked Jesus' claim to be the King of the Jews and jeered at His claims to be God.

Yet when Jesus appeared to the disciples, He invited them to look at the scars from what He'd been through. He didn't hide that part of his story from them; rather, those scars were a triumphant reminder!

Furthermore, Jesus didn't go into a long dialogue about how badly He'd been treated by the Roman soldiers. Instead He elevated triumph and redemption over the narrative of pain and loss. Jesus no longer suffered from His wounds, and He didn't waste his time or attention on those who had inflicted those wounds. He walked in victory.

In John 16:33, Jesus talks about the suffering that we encounter in life, but He also encourages us! Read that verse and write below what Jesus wants us to remember:

What about you? Do you still have wounds, or do you have scars? We've all been wounded by life. Some of our wounds are physical and evident, while others are emotional, relational, or spiritual and hidden deep inside.

Here's the thing: our wounds will heal according to how healthy we are.

- If your wounds are related to your beauty narrative, then those wounds will heal only to the extent that you've uncovered the details of your beauty narrative.
- If your wounds are shame-based, those wounds won't heal unless you deal with shame.
- If your wounds remain open because of unforgiveness, they won't heal until you forgive.

How will you know that your wounds are healing well and forming appropriate scars?

1. When you think about that painful circumstance as an event in the past, instead of carrying it around with you in your daily life.

Extra Insight:

These marks
tell a story…
They remind me of
Your Faithfulness
—Mandisa, "What
Scars Are For"[8]

Extra Insight:

Crown of Beauty: In Scripture, ancient people threw ashes on their heads to symbolize mourning. Through the prophet Isaiah's words (Isaiah 61: 1-3), we learn that the coming Messiah's work of redemption would relieve the Israelites' distress and that they would wear a beautiful crown on their heads.

2. When you've forgiven everyone involved who needs to be forgiven. (Remember, forgiveness is not the same as reconciliation.)
3. When you can celebrate the victory of overcoming in Jesus' name in spite of the heartache and pain that you've endured.
4. When you've healed enough to start sharing your story with others.

Long before Jesus went to the cross, He spoke through the prophet Isaiah and told God's chosen people about a time when they would be freed from spiritual captivity and the painful consequences of sin.

Read Isaiah 61:1-3. What would Jesus come to do for the suffering people?

Although the people felt that much had been lost, even destroyed, what did Jesus promise to give them? (v. 3)

Scars tell stories of pain and healing. Celebrate what Jesus has done for you by sharing your victory story.

Think about one aspect of your ugly struggle with beauty that you've taken steps to overcome through this Bible study. Tell your story by filling in the blanks:

I will never forget when _____

_____.

When this happened, I began to struggle with _____

_____.

For a long time, I felt/believed that _____

_____.

As a result of that struggle, I hated looking in the mirror because

_____.

Then one day I read the following verse (or story) in the Bible: _____.

I realized that _____.

Now I know God's truth, and I know I am healing from that painful part of my life because _____ _____.

While I still have the memories of that painful experience, God has healed my pain and given me _____ _____.

When I share my story with other women, I want to encourage them to remember _____ _____.

I love the idea that Jesus can heal us from the inside out! And healing is good news! So when we find healing, we need to tell someone about it. Think about this as you go throughout your day: How could the story of Jesus' healing in your life encourage another woman to turn to Jesus as well?

Live It Out

1. What is one thing that God impressed upon your heart during today's study?

2. What do you sense God leading you to think or do differently as a result of what you've studied?

Talk with God

Today should be a day of triumph! I hope that you've been able to see how God wants to take your story of healing and use your former ugly struggle with beauty to bring glory to His name. If you're not there yet, that's OK! You've got an outline for your story that I hope you're able to fill in soon. Regardless of where you're at, give God thanks for sending Jesus to heal your wounds and redeem your scars.

Day 4: Jesus Smells Good on You!

Beauty Mark
When we live by faith, our lives are a pleasing aroma to God.

Beauty Regimen

A research study published in *Science* magazine reported that humans can distinguish between an astonishing one trillion different smells! For a long time scientists believed that humans could distinguish between only ten thousand different smells, but testing revealed that our ability to smell is far greater than previously recognized.[9]

In addition to our tremendous ability to recognize smells, we can store and recall memories based on our sense of smell. Not only that, but our sense of smell also has the power to influence our mood and even impact our performance.[10]

During my junior year of high school, I dated a guy who loved to wear Polo cologne. In fact, the word *loved* might be an understatement considering how strong he smelled whenever we saw each other. Perhaps "heavily dunked" would be an appropriate description. While we were dating, I loved the scent too. But when we broke up, I couldn't stand it anymore. In fact, I had another friend who wore the same fragrance, and I stopped hanging out with him as well. Even though my friend was a great guy, the smell of that cologne brought back memories that I didn't want to remember.

Just as there are some smells I choose to avoid, there are other smells that I just adore, such as freshly baked chocolate chip cookies and fresh laundry. A deep draw of those scents instantly lifts my mood.

When my maternal grandmother passed away seven years ago, my mother and her sisters gave all of us grandkids an opportunity to choose a number of keepsakes. I chose just three things: my grandmother's handwritten recipe for her German chocolate cake and both bottles of her favorite perfume. Funny how I chose keepsakes with a strong sense of smell attached to them. Whenever I want to instantly remember her, I uncap one of those bottles of perfume and take a whiff. One sniff and my mind triggers dozens of memories of my grandmother. That olfactory sensation is so powerful that if I close my eyes, I can imagine she's there. The memories are so vivid that I rarely uncap that bottle to avoid being overwhelmed by the still-so-tender and deep sense of loss.

What's your favorite perfume or other scent? What sensations or memories are triggered when your nose picks up that scent?

Extra Insight:

"God is pleased by the aroma of sacrifice, whether a literal sacrifice or the figurative offering of Christian service."[11]

In Scripture, God uses our sense of smell and pleasing aromas as a metaphor to teach us about Himself and how we are to share the inner beauty that comes from Christ with the world.

Read 2 Corinthians 2:14-16. How does the Apostle Paul compare our lives to fragrance in this passage?

Paul says that our lives are a Christlike fragrance wafting up to God. He illustrates this point by using a Roman triumph or military parade as a framework. A Roman triumph was a grand procession of the Roman army that often took place after victory in a great campaign and featured the celebrated general or other military hero or public official. During a triumph, the Roman people would observe a processional of all the politicians, musicians, and spoils of the campaign, including the captured enemies and their weapons. In addition to the vast processional, garlands of flowers would hang on every shrine and incense would burn on every altar, giving off a heavily perfumed and fragrant scent throughout the entire proceeding.[12]

It might seem strange that we are described as captives in Christ's processional, but to be captives means that we are owned by Christ.

Look again at verse 14. What is the benefit of being a captive of Christ?

During the triumph, the smell of flowers and incense would be sweet to the victors but sickening to their enemies. Paul leverages this analogy to talk about how our aroma as Christ-followers might be perceived by those who accept Christ and those who reject Him.

Why would Paul describe the gospel message of Christ as a sweet perfume to those who accept Christ?

Why do nonbelievers dislike or reject our Christlike aroma?

At what point do you think someone might begin to appreciate the sweet scent of Christ?

God loves good aromas! How do we know this? In the Old Testament God commanded the Israelites to make specific kinds of sacrifices as atonement for their sins. When they performed the sacrifices in accordance with God's guidelines, those sacrifices pleased God. In fact, there is a particular phrase used often as a description of God's satisfaction.

Read Leviticus 1:9; 2:2; 23:18. What same two words are used each time (in your translation) to describe the scent rising up to God?

I don't know about you, but based on how often animal sacrifices are recorded in the Old Testament, I believe that God enjoys a good barbecue! Seriously, the importance of the sacrifice's aroma was not the smell but what the smell represents: Christ's death in our place. Though the Old Testament sacrifices were temporary and had to be repeated, Jesus became the ultimate and eternally pleasing sacrifice for us.

Read Ephesians 5:2 in the margin. What is Jesus' sacrifice for us described as?

How was Christ's sacrifice pleasing to God?

How does the Apostle Paul call us to follow Christ's example?

Extra Insight:

The alabaster bottle of perfume was valued around 300 denarii. Most day laborers only made a single denarius per day, so that alabaster bottle of perfume was worth nearly a year's wages.[13]

As followers of Christ, we are called to live a life a love—a beautiful representation of Christ's fragrant sacrifice for us. Mark 14 records a powerful story about a fragrant demonstration of love that happened just before Jesus' sacrifice on the cross.

Read Mark 14:1-9. What type of container did the woman bring into the house with her, and what was in that container?

What did she do with the perfume?

Why was she criticized by those around the table?

Earlier in our study we read in Luke 7 about an immoral woman who poured perfume on Jesus' feet and experienced peace and forgiveness (see Week 4 Day 3). However, that is not the same woman we find here in Mark 14. Though both events occurred in the home of a man named Simon, one was a Pharisee and the other was a man known for having had leprosy.

This woman in Mark 14 is believed to be Mary from Bethany, also known as Lazarus' sister. The nard she poured over Jesus' head was used in burial rituals. It was a rare and expensive perfume that people saved to purchase for their own funeral preparations, yet Mary poured out her entire supply on Jesus' head.

Imagine how strong the aroma would have been in that room! Perhaps the power of that familiar burial scent magnified Jesus' awareness of His impending crucifixion. Yet we must ask ourselves, Why would Mary make such a sacrifice? She wanted to serve Jesus with all that she had. That expensive bottle of perfume represented the best that she had. Mary gave her best to Jesus, and it was a pleasing aroma to him.

Reread Mark 14:6-9. What was Jesus' response to her critics?

What would it mean for you to be a "Christlike fragrance rising up to God" each day?

What are some clues that might indicate your life is giving off a Christlike fragrance? (Think about how your daily life and relationships might look, sound, or feel.)

As we close today, let me suggest three practical ways that each of our lives can be a sweet, Christlike fragrance to God on a daily basis:

1. *Stay connected to Christ.* If we are going to give off the fragrance of Christ, then we must stay connected to Him!
2. *Live obediently.* When we sacrifice our will so that God's will may be done in our lives, that sacrifice rises up to God as a sweet aroma. Whatever God is calling you to do, go ahead and do it.
3. *Live by faith.* Walking by faith isn't easy. There are many times when we're not sure what to do next, but we can always count on God to lead us. Follow after God, and He will take care of what's before you.

Sweet friend, when you are an aroma to God, you will be a beautiful blessing to others as well.

Live It Out

1. **What is one thing that God impressed upon your heart during today's study?**

2. What do you sense God leading you to think or do differently
   as a result of what you've studied?

Talk with God

As you reflect on today's Live It Out questions, allow them to be inspiration for a time of prayer. My prayer is that your life will be a sweet, Christlike fragrance rising up to God and spreading to all around you.

Day 5: "For Now" Is Not "Forever"

Beauty Mark
God takes care of us, so that we can take care of ourselves.

Beauty Regimen

Once at a women's conference I was attending, the speaker was talking about being a woman. She looked at the women in the audience and said: "Ladies, if the barn needs painting, then paint it!" The women erupted into a loud cheer. Meanwhile I was confused, looking around and wondering, *Where's the barn that we're talking about here?*

I soon discovered that the barn represented us. What the speaker meant was that it's OK for us to take care of us. She gave us permission to take care of our bodies and take time for ourselves.

Having grown up in the suburbs, it took me a while to understand why a barn was an appropriate analogy. Luckily, I married a country boy and could reflect on what I've learned about barns through the years.

My husband's family lives in the rural northwestern part of Ohio, so when we drive out to visit his family, we pass at least one hundred barns along the way. We see big barns, small barns, and every size in between. I love classic red barns. These large structures with bold colors and simple lines remind me of some of my favorite childhood books such as *Charlotte's Web* and *The Little House* books. The barns in those books were as much a part of the story as the characters themselves.

My heart saddens at the sight of a big, old, dilapidated barn. Once upon a time that barn was new and glorious. Imagine it with me. The proud farmer and his wife are standing in front of the barn they sacrificed to build. There's a tear in the farmer's eye as he envisions that barn as security for his family's future. That new barn will hold their precious livestock and keep their harvest dry. That barn represents the hopes and dreams of generations.

Fast forward to the present. The farmer and his wife are now standing before the old, dilapidated barn. They never imagined a day when that barn would start to deteriorate. Perhaps money was tight, so the farmer couldn't replace busted wood planks or patch the roof. At some point, however, I'm sure the farmer realized that his barn was starting to look tired and worn. I'm also sure he spent years quietly promising himself the same thing over and over again: *I'll take care of it one of these days.* Unfortunately, that day never came.

How often have you put off caring for yourself, believing that once you take care of everything for everyone else, then you can do something for yourself? How many times have you said, "Oh, I would love to do that—someday."

> *Someday, I'll have lunch with _____.*
> *Someday, I'll work out regularly.*
> *Someday, I'll update my haircut.*
> *Someday, I'll take a vacation.*

What's your "someday"?

Someday, I'll _____.

Why don't we let someday be *now*? I can answer that question with one word: guilt.

For some of us, guilt is our default emotion. In fact, we've felt guilty for so long that it has become like a comfortable pair of old, worn jeans. We know we should take them off and burn them, but we're used to wearing them and there's not a compelling reason to stop.

How do we stop living in guilt and embrace God's freedom? What would it look and feel like for you to care for your physical, emotional, spiritual, and relational needs without guilt? That's what we're diving into today, and I'm expecting God to show up and show you something new that brings hope and freedom to your current situation!

Using a barn as a metaphor for how we care for ourselves, how's your barn looking lately?

Chips and cracks are an early indicator that the structure isn't as sound as before. Are there any areas of your life—emotional, physical, or spiritual—that are starting to chip or crack?

King Solomon reigned from around 970 BC to 930 BC. Known as the wisest man who ever lived, he had unmatched brilliance. Yet he entered the final years of his reign disillusioned by all he had known. The Book of Ecclesiastes records some of the lessons that Solomon learned.

Read Ecclesiastes 3:1-11. What does King Solomon recognize about life in these verses?

List all of the experiences named in these verses that you've had over the past few months.

Are there any named that you should have experienced but haven't? If so, why not?

There are many things I love about this passage. Notice that there are God-ordained seasons to our lives. Our lives never stay the same, no matter how hard we try to control or regulate our lifestyles. Unexpected joys and sorrows find us at various times. Yet even with the unexpected, there is still an underlying flow to our lives. Many have described the four seasons of life in the context of the four seasons of weather:

- Winter—a time to reflect inwardly and learn
- Spring—a time of new birth and new beginnings
- Summer—a time of growth, enjoyment, and celebration
- Fall—a time of transition and change[14]

Which season describes your life right now? What are some of the events you are experiencing in this season?

What impact is this season of life having on your desire or ability to care for yourself—internally and externally? Are you giving more attention to one than the other?

Where does our guilt or the difficulty we have caring for ourselves stem from? Expectations. As women, we can have unreasonable expectations for ourselves. We've talked about some of those unfair outer-beauty expectations, but we also have certain unreasonable performance expectations.

Last year I received a gift certificate for a free massage. I love massages! However, I drove around with that gift certificate in my purse for six months because I felt guilty about using it. Well, I didn't steal the gift certificate, so why did I feel so guilty? Here were my reasons:

- I hadn't filed a necessary homeowner insurance claim,
- I hadn't completed some papers for health insurance reimbursement,
- I hadn't picked up the dog's heartworm medicine, and
- I hadn't scheduled my mammogram.

Since my list of performance failures loomed large in my mind, I didn't believe that I deserved that massage until the tasks on that list were completed. So that gift certificate stayed in my purse for half a year until I finally gave myself permission to use it, even though I hadn't performed up to my expectations.

Perhaps you can't relate, knowing that you would have used that gift certificate immediately! But no doubt there are other areas in your life where your own expectations can interfere with self-care.

Now it's your turn in the hot seat! What are some of the expectations you have for yourself that you are struggling to meet?

How do you treat yourself when you don't meet your personal expectations?

When it comes to caring for ourselves, guilt can impede or arrest our good intentions. As long as there is someone else in our lives to care for, we often are tempted to put ourselves at the back of the line. Friends, when will we understand that caring for ourselves and caring for others are not mutually exclusive? If we can multitask in other areas of our lives, surely we can figure this out. We don't have to abandon our obligations or those we love in order to take care of ourselves. And we don't have to feel guilty about it either.

How do we reset the expectations of our lives to that we can live in freedom rather than guilt?

In 1 Corinthians 6, the Apostle Paul challenges us with the realization that our bodies do not belong to ourselves but to God.

Read 1 Corinthians 6:19-20 in the margin. What is the price that God paid for our bodies?

What are the things we need to do in order to honor God with our bodies?

What are some of the things you need to avoid in order to honor God?

Two of the main culprits for not taking care of ourselves are stress and worry. When we're in a busy or difficult season, we tend to look out for everyone around us, and the ones we stop looking out for are us. Yet God doesn't want worry to warp our perspective.

Read 1 Peter 5:7 in the margin. What should we do with our worries and cares?

> [19] Don't you realize that your body is the temple of the Holy Spirit, who lives in you and was given to you by God? You do not belong to yourself, [20] for God bought you with a high price. So you must honor God with your body.
> (1 Corinthians 6:19-20)

> *Give* all your *worries* and cares to God, for he cares about you.
> (1 Peter 5:7, *emphasis added*)

In other translations, the word for "give" is *cast*, which means throwing our worries to God. How hard is it for you to give your worries over to God?

What happens to our hearts and minds when we give our worries to God instead of carrying them around?

What are some potential spiritual consequences that might arise from constant worry and lack of physical self-care?

When we realize that God cares for us, then we are able to care for ourselves! We don't have to try to solve every problem that comes into our lives or the lives of those we care about.

As we cast our cares to God and care for ourselves, our inner beauty has a chance to shine through. As people observe the challenges in our lives, they won't expect us to be perfect, but we can inspire them by our faithfulness to a God who cares for us in every season.

Live It Out

1. What is one thing that God impressed upon your heart during today's study?

2. What do you sense God leading you to think or do differently as a result of what you've studied?

Talk with God

I encourage you to immediately release any guilty feelings that might have surfaced during today's study. The purpose of this lesson was to help free you from guilt and give you permission to take care of yourself in a way that honors God and allows His inner beauty to radiate outward. If you're still struggling with guilt about self-care—which is essential to healing and wholeness—then by all means, talk with God about it today. If you're doing well in this area, then devote precious time to praying for another woman—perhaps a friend, family member, or someone in your group—who may be struggling. You don't need to confront her, but you can pray for God's increasing influence in her life in this area.

WINNING OUR UGLY STRUGGLE

Yet God has made _____ beautiful for its own time. He has planted eternity in the human heart, but even so, people cannot see the whole scope of God's work from beginning to end. (Ecclesiastes 3:11)

When we start feeling overwhelmed by certain situations, it's very easy for us to stop taking care of _____.

_____ *all your worries and cares to God, for he cares about you. (1 Peter 5:7)*

Some translations use the word *cast*, which means throw. We are literally to throw our cares at God.

Give your burdens to the Lord,
and he will take care of you.
He will not permit the godly to slip and fall.
(Psalm 55:22)

When you realize that God _____ about you, you don't have to feel guilty _____ about yourself.

Caring for myself didn't mean that I was _____ someone else.
Caring for myself allowed me to care for others _____.

How are you caring for yourself today?

No matter the season of your life, God is present with you. God will take care of you so that you can take care of yourself.

Week 6

DISCOVERING YOUR BEAUTY BALANCE

Memory Verse

[25] She is clothed with strength and dignity,
  and she laughs without fear of the future.
[26] When she speaks, her words are wise,
  and she gives instructions with kindness. (Proverbs 31:25-26)

This Week's Theme

Finding our beauty balance gives us freedom to live and love.

I love watching gymnastics on television. However, there's one event that always puts me on the edge of my seat: the balance beam. Athletes spring into the air, landing on a padded, aluminum beam only four inches wide. My size 11 feet would dwarf such a narrow base, yet those nimble athletes perform sophisticated acrobatic sequences requiring them to flip, jump, or straddle the narrow apparatus.

Sometimes an athlete will complete a maneuver and wobble atop the beam. In order to regain and realign, the gymnast will complete a "balance check," throwing her arms out from her sides and struggling against gravity for stability.

While most of us balance standing firmly with both feet on the ground, gymnasts find balance in all sorts of positions. Balance doesn't always mean equality. Sometimes gymnasts will balance on one leg or carefully on one arm. To gain balance, the athletes must shift their weight proportionally and hold their body in the desired balanced position.

Balance isn't just 50/50; it's also a matter of proportion.

Cooking provides another great example of this concept. When cooking, it is important to make sure that flavors are balanced even though the amounts may not be in equal proportions. Some flavors are more potent than others, so mixing them in equal amounts would not have the desired impact. Pure vanilla added in small amounts magnifies the yum-factor of most cookies or cakes but would ruin the recipe if added in equal measure to the milk. There are times in life when balance doesn't mean equality but rather proportionality.

Both illustrations are helpful as we review what inner and outer beauty look like together in the correct proportions. I call this the "beauty balance."

You'll notice in the drawing that inner beauty is weightier (and hence hangs lower) than outer beauty. I like to say that inner beauty matters most, but it's not the only thing that matters. While inner beauty should be emphasized more than physical beauty, it doesn't provide the entire picture of beauty.

This visual reinforces the idea that both kinds of beauty have their place as long as we cultivate them in the right balance. This week we will explore what it means to be a woman who CARES about outer beauty while achieving the right balance or proportion to inner beauty.

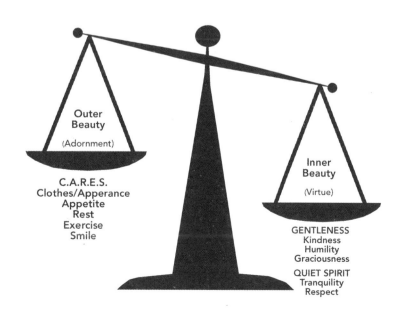

Day 1: Becoming a Woman Who CARES—Clothes

Beauty Mark
Our clothes are a reflection of our attitude, beliefs, and character.

Beauty Regimen

I love clothes, and I love that the Bible talks about clothes. Have you noticed how often the Bible mentions what people were wearing? In Genesis, Adam and Eve scrambled to cover their bodies after they sinned. A whole lot of drama went down after the flood when Noah passed out after drinking too much and one of his sons didn't cover him properly. In Leviticus, God gave specific instructions to the Israelites about how clothing should be made and what types of material should be avoided. Even greater instruction was given for how the priests' clothing should be constructed and made.

Clothing references abound in both the Old and New Testaments, and we see that clothing is more than just a covering.

- Biblical figures would tear their clothing as a sign of grief. (Genesis 37:34; 2 Samuel 3:31; Joel 2:13)
- Clothing was given as a gift. For example, Jacob gave Joseph a coat, and there was an ancient tradition of giving sets of clothing as gifts. (Genesis 37:3)
- Clothing was put on those in authority as a symbol of their power and position. For example, Queen Esther dressed in her royal robes before going to see King Xerxes. (Esther 5:1)
- In the New Testament, Paul used body coverings such as shoes and belts and armor as an analogy for preparing ourselves for spiritual battle. (Ephesians 6:10-18)

Clothing was—and still is—an expression of our human experience. Clothing is communication. What we put on our bodies speaks its own language to the people around us. God told Samuel that people look at the outward appearance (1 Samuel 16:7), which means that people observe how we look, what we wear, and how we express ourselves through our style and then draw conclusions about who we are based on what they see. While God acknowledges our human tendencies, His focus is on the condition and bent of our hearts. Frankly, we would do well to follow

God's example and reserve our deepest passion for caring for the inner life of others, rather than be overly concerned with their outer appearance.

If God judges the heart, is clothing a spiritual topic, then? In a sense, yes. Because our bodies are created by God and we are called by God to be holy in all that we say and do, this means there is a spiritual element to the clothing that we wear. Furthermore, it's up to us to understand how the clothes we wear are a reflection of our ABCs: attitude, beliefs, and character.

There are lots of voices telling us how we should look and dress, so what are the questions we need to ask ourselves about our clothes? Let's look at three questions that can help to define the "why" behind what we choose to buy and how we dress ourselves each day. As we browse through the store racks, search online, and evaluate what we already own, we can ask ourselves these questions:

1. Personality	2. Sensitivity	3. Dignity
Am I wearing clothes that reflect my belief that I am beautiful?	Am I wearing clothes that are appropriate for this particular situation?	Do the clothes on my body reflect my desire to live for the glory of God and to bless others, including myself?

Your answers to these questions will be personal and specific to your own life situation, but let's look together at several scriptural principles that can help us to discover godly convictions about what we buy and wear.

1. Personality: Am I wearing clothes that reflect my belief that I am beautiful?

What we wear often reflects our attitudes and beliefs about ourselves, as well as how we want other people to see us. Is it possible for us to dress in a way that contradicts how we feel about ourselves? Of course! But over a long period of time, our beliefs about who we are and what is important to us will manifest themselves through what we wear.

As a curvy girl who loves Jesus, I want to dress so that people can look me in the eye and feel comfortable talking about Jesus with me. I never want my clothes to confuse people about who I am and what I am living for. Each of us will have differing clothing convictions based on our stage of life, body type, and most of all, God's leading for us.

If you get a chance, go through your closet and prayerfully ask God if there are any articles of clothing that you need to donate or simply remove from circulation. I'm not just talking about clothes that may be revealing but also clothes that are worn out, ripped, ill-fitting, or simply make you sad when you wear them.

One of the keys to knowing what to buy and wear is knowing who you are in Christ. Your identity as a beautiful woman rooted in Christ serves as a helpful filter when you shop and get dressed.

What is your general attitude about clothes? What are some words you would use to describe the clothes in your closet?

Do you think that the clothes you wear most often fit your personality? If not, why do you think there is a gap between what you wear and how you see yourself?

We all have different personalities, and when we dress according to those personalities, we look natural and comfortable. This affirms how God has created us in His image as unique creations. Your clothing is part of expressing who you are and the fact that you are beautiful already! The clothes won't make you beautiful, but they will highlight your God-given beauty.

For me, I love wearing classic colors and styles. I discovered this about myself in college. I have artistic friends who love wearing loose and flowy fabrics. Other friends are casual and enjoy plaids and khakis. Your style and personality should go together, and it's okay for you to spend some time discovering your preferences.

2. Sensitivity: Am I wearing clothes that are appropriate for this particular situation?

We have different races, cultures, backgrounds, and individual perspectives. God created us to be unique. Yet our God-given uniqueness should not overtake our call to holy living or our desire to be a light for Christ in our world.

When we possess sensitivity, we recognize that although we are in control of what we wear, our choices have an impact on others. When in doubt, I always overdress for a situation. This simply means that if I'm unsure about what to wear, I choose to look as nice as seems reasonably appropriate. I'm not talking about a floor-length gown but an outfit that I'd wear to look nice at work. It's much better to be overdressed than underdressed!

Read 1 Corinthians 10:23-24 in the margin. Here Paul addresses a group of Christians who proclaim Jesus Christ but want to keep

operating as if nothing in their lives has changed. How does Paul challenge their attitude?

How does this verse apply to our clothing choices? What kind of tension is created when we dress in a manner that is contrary to our faith?

In this passage, Paul addresses the topic of Christian liberty and gives his audience an important lesson: "just because you can doesn't mean you should." In regards to our clothing choices, we might think about being careful not to wear a low-cut top or an ultra-short skirt. I like to say that as women, we have "bells and whistles." How we dress in a situation dictates how much attention we'll draw with our clothes. It's one thing for people to politely nod as we walk by, but it's another for people to gawk or whisper because our clothes are unflattering, unkempt, too tight, or too revealing.

Paul's words also apply to giving attention and care to our appearance. While it's allowable to wear sweatpants and old T-shirts every day, it's probably not beneficial. Sure, you can wear that outfit every day, but when you look in the mirror, how are your heart and mind impacted by the bare-basics effort you put into caring for the body that God gave you? Yes, there are seasons in life when sweats and a T-shirt are the best that we can do on a regular basis, but that should be the case for certain seasons of life—not for a lifetime.

What are some of your personal boundaries when it comes to dressing? What are some things that you refrain from wearing because it could be offensive or distracting to others?

Here are a few practical tips for dressing with sensitivity:

1. Know your surroundings. If you are dressing for a new experience, check online for photos of a similar past event, make a phone call in advance, or find out what the hostess will be wearing.
2. Ask for feedback. If you are wearing something for the first time, ask a trusted friend or family member for advice on how the outfit looks.

3. Listen to the crowd. This isn't about looking for acceptance from others. Rather, pay attention to comments or nonverbal communication about what you are wearing. If you're getting catcalls or lots of stares, then the outfit may not be appropriate. Likewise, if you never receive compliments about anything you wear, it may be time to update your wardrobe.

I recognize that this section might have touched some sensitive places in your heart. As you reflect on dressing with sensitivity, please remember that God loves you as you are. Your clothes should never be a source of shame or condemnation!

3. Dignity: Do the clothes on my body reflect my desire to live for the glory of God...?

Modesty is a word used frequently in Scripture with regard to women and clothing. Though I absolutely agree with the scriptural principle of modesty, the term unfortunately is often associated with words such as *frumpy* and *outdated*. Modesty is generally described as dressing in a way that doesn't draw attention to one's body or cause the opposite sex to objectify one's body.

For practical purposes, I like to use the phrase "dressing with dignity" coined by author Colleen Hammond. The word *dignity* means worthy of honor or respect.[1] So when we dress with dignity, we dress in a way that causes people to honor and respect us for how we appear to them. This is not the kind of honor and respect that elevates us above others but the kind that reflects who God created us to be.

Read Proverbs 11:22 in the margin. What word is used here to mean "modesty"?

To understand this verse, remember that pigs are known for using their noses to root around in the dirt and mud. Metal rings were put in their noses to prevent them from rooting up the earth.[2]

Why is a beautiful woman who lacks discretion or modesty likened to a gold ring in a pig's nose?

In 1 Timothy, Paul was writing to Timothy, who was headed out to correct some issues in the Ephesian church. Ephesus was a city filled with many wealthy citizens, and the women were known for dressing in an extravagant and sensual manner. Among other things, Paul was writing to Timothy to provide counsel on how to instruct the women to dress with dignity.

Read 1 Timothy 2:9-10. What were some of the instructions that Paul gave for how women should dress?

Paul wasn't telling the ladies to stop styling their hair or wearing jewelry. Rather, he challenged the ladies to draw their attention to God rather than draw attention from others. Instead of a "look at me" mentality that aims to glorify self, our mind-set should reflect a "daughter of the King" attitude.

How would you explain the difference between dressing attractively and dressing sensually or seductively?

The most objective way to identify whether or not an image is seductive is the amount of skin that is showing or the tightness of the clothing around our chest, hips, or behind. In our image-driven social media culture, it's not hard to find photos of women dressed seductively, trying to draw attention to themselves by showcasing their feminine features.

There's a popular saying that has been attributed to various people: "What gets rewarded gets repeated." The truth is that pictures of women dressed seductively often reap more feedback than pictures of women dressed non-seductively. That feedback comes in the form of "likes," comments, and dollars.

There are women who have been trafficked or forced into industries requiring seductive dress in order to draw dollars from customers, and we must band together as women to push against those industries and stand up for the dignity of our sisters. However, this conversation about dressing with dignity is targeted at the need for us to discern the motives of our own hearts: Am I dressing for God or people?

The need to dress with dignity also applies to women who may have let themselves go. While I know that living with small children can be tough and caring for elderly family members doesn't leave a lot of time for personal care, it is important to consider whether or not you are dressing with dignity. In busy or stressful seasons of life, it can be easy for us to just give up on our physical appearance, but I want to challenge you today to

Charm is deceptive, and beauty does not last; but a woman who fears the Lord will be greatly praised. (Proverbs 31:30)

dress yourself with dignity, even if no one else is around to see it but you and God.

The ultimate aim of dressing modestly and dressing with dignity is to point people to God rather than to point people to ourselves.

Read Proverbs 31:30 in the margin. In this verse, *beauty* refers to physical or outer beauty. What is given the greatest value in this verse?

When it comes to the clothes in your closet, nothing you own will last forever. Our clothes are temporary coverings that we drape over our temporary bodies. This is why Proverbs 31:30 offers such great wisdom for us not to be *overly* focused on our physical bodies (though we shouldn't ignore them) but to put our focus on God. I love how pastor and author John Piper breaks down the meaning of "fear the Lord" for us: "A woman who fears the Lord will not run away from God to satisfy her longings and relieve her anxieties. She will wait for the Lord. She will hope in God. She will stay close to the heart of God and trust in his promises."[3]

Whenever you are making clothing choices, think about personality, sensitivity, and dignity and the three questions we've explored today. They will help you to prioritize God's perspective rather than the opinions of culture, which will help you to find peace, freedom, and victory in your ugly struggle with beauty.

Live It Out

1. What is one thing that God impressed upon your heart during today's study?

2. What do you sense God leading you to think or do differently as a result of what you've studied?

Talk with God

What we wear is personal, and God wants to speak to us individually. If you can, head over to your closet for today's prayer time with God. As you stand there looking at your clothes, ask God to reveal those items that don't reflect your personality, embrace sensitivity, or allow you to dress with dignity. (If you aren't sure what you're hearing from God, repeat this exercise with a trusted Christian friend.) Express to God your desire and commitment to dress with modesty and dignity so that you may bring glory to Him.

Day 2: Becoming a Woman Who CARES—Appetite

Beauty Mark
Our biggest appetite should be a hunger for God.

Beauty Regimen

The next step to becoming a woman who CARES is learning how to manage appetite. We're not going to talk about eating certain foods or following a particular diet plan. Appetite is much more sophisticated than diets or calories, even though those elements are involved in the discussion.

God designed our bodies to experience hunger, and He created food sources for us to consume in order for our bodies to function. However, appetite is different from hunger:

> Hunger: Physiological need for food
> Appetite: Psychological desire for food [4]

I don't know about you, but sometimes it can be tough for me to distinguish between my *need* for food and my *desire* to eat. Without being critical of my body size, I'm fairly certain that quite a bit of what I consume isn't related to a biological need for food.

A couple of years ago, my friend Jera made a pecan pie for me. I love pecan pie! I took that pie into my house and set it on the counter. While I wasn't physically hungry, that pie started to look really good to me. In fact, I could hear that pie talking to me. Seriously, it was! It said, "Barb, I'm over here. It's so lonely over here. I think I'd like to be in your tummy much more than I'd like to be sitting on this counter."

I tried not to listen to that pie, but it kept talking. The only way for me to quiet the pie was to eat it. So I did. I ate the *entire* pie in one afternoon.

Are you horrified? Trust me, I was—especially since I wasn't even hungry. So what happened? My appetite, that's what happened!

God created our bodies to need food. However, God gave us appetites as well. In addition to an appetite for food, we are born with an appetite for

Appetite comes
with eating;
the more one has,
the more one
would have.
—French proverb

love, acceptance, satisfaction, achievement, and connection. Think about those things you long for every day, such as someone to love, acceptance by others, or a deep sense of connection. Each of those things represents a craving or an appetite.

The fact that we have appetites is neither bad nor good; however, everything rides on how we will satisfy those appetites when they arise. How you manage your desire for love, acceptance, achievement, and connection determines whether you are controlling your appetite or your appetite is controlling you.

As women, this concept is critical because we often have unfulfilled appetites; and when our craving for love, acceptance, or connection goes unfulfilled, we often turn to food in order to temporarily satisfy that unmet need. Does the term "comfort food" sound familiar? We use it to refer to those favorite foods we seek to fill the painful void inside us.

If I'm having a really bad day at work—the kind of day when I don't feel appreciated, valued, or successful—a hollow, deep pit begins to form within me and shout for satisfaction. Perhaps you've heard it before: "Gimme, gimme! I'll take whatever you've got!"

How often do we toss into that void a half dozen cookies or a carton of ice cream? One of my favorite quotes is from character Lavon Hayes in the CW television network show *Hart of Dixie*. After his girlfriend breaks up with him, Lavon shows up on his friend's doorstep with a bag of donuts and says, "Help me eat my feelings."[5]

When the signals cross between our hunger and our appetite, our bodies pay the price because we use food—and other consumables such as alcohol or drugs—in a manner that harms us.

Are you experiencing a "void" right now? If so, what unmet needs or appetites are you longing to satisfy?

We learn about the danger of appetite from the Old Testament story of twin brothers Jacob and Esau. These two struggled against each other in their mother's womb during her entire pregnancy, and their struggle continued throughout much of their lives. At birth, Esau emerged first, followed by Jacob, who was born holding onto his brother's heel. In fact, Jacob's name actually means "heel grabber."[6]

As the twins grew up, Esau became a skillful hunter and enjoyed the great outdoors, while Jacob liked being close to home. However, Jacob loved the food that his brother brought home for the family to eat.

One day, Esau arrived home proclaiming that he was starving, and he demanded some of the stew that Jacob was cooking.

Read Genesis 25:31-34. What did Jacob ask for in return for giving Esau food? (v. 31)

What did Esau proclaim in verse 32? If he was a skillful hunter, could this have been true?

Why do you think that Esau would trade the birthright—something so valuable—for a bowl of stew, which was only temporary?

Even though Esau had relinquished something so valuable, what did he do after eating the bowl of stew? (v. 34)

Extra Insight:

In ancient times, the oldest son's birthright was a prized possession. A birthright meant that the eldest son would become the family's leader, and he was entitled to a double-portion of the inheritance.[7]

It is tempting to judge Esau for such a rash, foolish decision, but we've all experienced something similar. This story in Genesis 25 may feature a bowl of stew, but what happened had nothing to do with food. The tragedy of Esau's situation had everything to do with his appetite. Esau was in no danger of dying from starvation, yet something deep inside of him was hollow and empty enough to feel like hunger.

We women are notorious emotional eaters. When our hunger for stability, healing, peace, acceptance, or love goes unsatisfied, we often seek satisfaction in food.

How often do you eat when you feel bad—about yourself or your situation? Mark an X on the line below.

1_____10
Never   Always

What kinds of foods do you pick up and have difficulty putting down when you are hurting?

How would you say you manage your unmet appetites most often? Circle one:

Healthy behaviors   Unhealthy behaviors

While Jesus was fully divine, He was also fully human, which means that He had to deal with hunger and appetites. In Matthew 4, we read how Satan used Jesus' hunger and appetite to tempt Him to forsake God for selfish gain.

Read Matthew 4:1-4.

How long did Jesus go without food? (v. 2)

What did Satan suggest to Jesus? (v. 3)

Jesus could have turned those stones into bread at any point. He didn't need Satan's prompting. He realized that Satan was using His physical hunger to attempt to trigger an appetite for significance. Notice that Satan said, "If you are the Son of God…" (v. 3). After struggling with such hunger, Jesus could have used His divine power to meet both a need and a desire, but He knew that a temporary solution wouldn't cure the greater spiritual need.

What was Jesus' response to Satan? (v. 4)

The words that Jesus quoted were from Deuteronomy 8:3. Jesus was acknowledging that our spiritual need is greater than our physical need, and the solution is not food but dependence on God and God's Word. While our need for food is ever present, we must not confuse our physical hunger with our deepest hunger in life.

So how should we manage our appetites? What are some practical steps we can take? There are many, but I'd like us to consider just three.

1. Understand your current physical and emotional state.

The acronym HALT stands for hungry, angry, lonely, and tired.[8] This term, which is used often in recovery circles, reminds us to be aware of how our physical and emotional condition can impact our ability to make wise choices.

If you think about the times when you struggle most with the desire for love, acceptance, satisfaction, achievement, or connection, it's often when you're also struggling with one of the HALT conditions. For example, if I don't sleep well and then I have an argument with my husband, my lack of sleep amplifies the loss of connection I feel. Or if you get cut off in traffic, making you late to work, and then you are called out by your boss for a mistake on a project, your sense of failure is amplified by the anger caused by the drive into work.

If left unchecked, your appetite can control your relationship with food. But when you are aware of your physical and emotional condition, then you can remind yourself that food won't fill that deep void; only dependence on God will. That brings us to step 2.

2. Practice dependence on God.

In Matthew 4:4, Jesus told Satan that the key to satisfaction is dependence on God. This is true for each of us. None of our greatest problems was ever solved by eating a carton of ice cream or bringing home cartons of Chinese food. I've tried!

Earlier in our study we learned how important it is to "see God first" when we look in the mirror. We can apply that same principle when our appetite starts chirping like a baby bird waiting for its mama to return. In that moment we can open up the Bible—or call on our GPS (God Positioning Scriptures)—see God's words, and allow those words to sink into that deep void, filling it in a way that peanut-butter-chocolate-buckeye brownies never could!

When we open the Bible, we see:

- God's promises for our lives,
- God's faithfulness in all circumstances, and
- God's great love for us!

What if we could use God's promises as a springboard to propel us away from emotional eating toward filling ourselves with God? When we combine Scripture and prayer, the combination can—and does—fill us up!

3. Phone a friend!

Once we have recognized our current condition and have practiced dependence on God by reminding ourselves of the promises and truths of Scripture and calling out to Him in prayer, then it's appropriate and helpful to look to friends for extra reinforcement. God has created us to live in community, and our Christian friends are great sources of encouragement and support. They want us to experience God's joy and peace in life.

So once you've looked to God and listened to what He has to say about your longing for love, acceptance, significance, satisfaction, or achievement, that is a good time to phone a mature Christian friend and share your struggle.

In some situations, especially if you've struggled with a particular appetite for a long time, you also may find it beneficial or necessary to seek the help of a pastor or counselor. If a trusted friend or loved one suggests you seek professional help, always accept that as the loving, well-meaning advice it is intended to be.

As you consider these three ways to manage your appetite, what are some action steps you need to consider taking in your life?

What might your life look and feel like in three months if you took those action steps?

Who can help to hold you accountable?

Discovering and dealing with our emotional hunger can truly transform our lives! If this has been a struggle for you, I challenge you to create your action plan and dream about the future. What would your life look like if you satisfied your deepest hungers with God rather than food or anything else? Oh, what a blessing you would experience!

Live It Out

1. What is one thing that God impressed upon your heart during today's study?

2. What do you sense God leading you to think or do differently as a result of what you've studied?

Talk with God

Ask God to help you develop the sensitivity to know the difference between the *need* for food and the *desire* for food. If you are struggling with an unfulfilled appetite, tell God about how that unfulfilled desire makes you feel. Invite God to fill that empty void with His love and peace.

Day 3: Becoming a Woman Who CARES—Rest

Beauty Mark
We are blessed when we rest.

Beauty Regimen

Take a moment to think about how the creation of the world must have been from God's perspective. At first there was nothing, and then, shazaam! Each day God created different elements of our world. Not only did God create from nothing but He also designed different colors and species to provide an array of diversity in our world.

While God never grows tired, we do! Life tires us out. These days life feels nonstop for most of us, and all of the movement around us adds to the tiredness we feel.

In 1930, British economist John Maynard Keynes theorized that future generations would need to work only fifteen hours per week in order to support their families. At the time, Keynes believed that the rate of manufacturing and technological advances would become so efficient that we all would need to work less.[9]

Except things didn't quite work out as Keynes proposed.

While technology permeates every area of our lives, the efficiencies of all the advances actually have increased the pace of our lives rather than slowed it down. While we may not have to bake bread from scratch or wash our clothes by hand on a washboard, the constant activity and digital communication around us makes us feel very busy.

One day I asked my friends on Facebook to rate how busy they feel on a scale of 1-10, with 1 being "not at all" and 10 being "crazy!"[10] In a few hours, more than one hundred people chimed in with their answer. When I averaged their responses, the average answer was 20.19, which was well over the top number of 10 that I had given. So I started looking at their responses. Here are a few:

12
100 (This was a popular answer!)
357.2
80

One person wrote "three hundred thousand quadrillion." I didn't know how many zeros were needed for that answer, so I didn't add that response into the average. The bottom line is that people today feel busy, rushed, weary, and tired.

What about you? How busy do you *feel*? Circle a number below.

1	2	3	4	5	6	7	8	9	10
(Not at all)									(Crazy!)

What are some of the reasons for your answer?

What happens when we feel overly busy and tired? How does it impact our lives—specifically our ability to care for our bodies?

In December 2000, I left a successful career in pharmaceutical sales to become an executive director for a nonprofit. Over the next nine months, I worked six or seven days a week trying to raise money and develop relationships with potential donors. While I had the opportunity to bring my youngest daughter to work with me, I rarely saw her during my ten- to twelve-hour work days. I almost missed seeing the first time she crawled, and she was only ten steps away from my office.

By August 2001, I started to burn out. My husband recognized it before I did. While I desired to do my best, I overran my physical resources, and the rest of my life started to unravel as a result. My short-term memory failed, I cried often, and I didn't sleep well. I was anxious about my performance, believing that if I worked hard enough I could find a way to excel. Yet the more effort that I poured into my work, the more anxious and stressed that I became at work and home.

By December of that year I was completely burned out and needed to leave the organization because I had nothing left to offer. In fact, it took almost three years for me to recover from the physical and emotional burnout.

What happened? I never took time to rest and, instead, pushed my body beyond tired to constant exhaustion. I stopped leaving regular, rhythmic space for God to speak into my life and correct my dangerous path.

We experience so many different demands on our bodies and physical resources on a regular basis. While our hearts and minds know that we can't be everything to everyone, that often doesn't stop us from trying. However, only God can go 24-7 without rest; we cannot.

Friends, burnout is not beautiful. Neither are bags under our eyes or nerves that are frayed because we've been stretched far beyond what's reasonable. We must take time to rest. We see the importance of rest from the very beginning.

In Genesis 1, we read that God demonstrated His tremendous power by creating the universe. Then in Genesis 2 we learn that as soon as God finished creation, He intentionally took a break—but not because He was tired. God never grows weary, but He does model for us the importance of stopping to reflect on our work.

Read Genesis 2:2-3 in the margin. What do these verses tell us about the seventh day? How did God define or describe that day of rest?

When God stopped working, He declared that pause from work to be holy, or set apart. God could have kept working, but He didn't because He wanted to define and model an important spiritual principle for our lives.

God would later give His people specific instructions about rest. While giving Moses the Ten Commandments to guide the newly freed Israelites after hundreds of years in captivity in Egypt, God included these words:

[8]"Remember to observe the Sabbath day by keeping it holy. [9]You have six days each week for your ordinary work, [10]but the seventh day is a Sabbath day of rest dedicated to the Lord your God. On that day no one in your household may do any work. This includes you, your sons and daughters, your male and female servants, your livestock, and any foreigners living among you." (Exodus 20:8-10)

[2]On the seventh day God had finished his work of creation, so he rested from all his work. [3]And God blessed the seventh day and declared it holy, because it was the day when he rested from all his work of creation. (Genesis 2:2-3)

Extra Insight:

"God did not rest as one weary, but as one well pleased."[11]

Circle the words *Sabbath* and *ordinary work* in the passage on the previous page. What kinds of ordinary work did God call the Israelites to stop on the Sabbath?

The Hebrew word for *Sabbath* is *Sabbat* (also *Shabbat*), which appears to come from the verb *sabat* (also *shavat*), meaning to stop or cease.[12] Considering that the Israelites had spent hundreds of years as slaves, they needed to establish a new rhythm to their lives. While slavery dictated that they must work according to the mandates of their captors, God wanted to set a new pace for their lives. Rather than working constantly, God wanted the Israelites to have downtime to remember all that God provided for them. Not only that, but out of great love for His people, God wanted to bless them by giving them space to care for their hearts, minds, and bodies.

On a scale of 1 to 10, how tired do you feel lately? Make an X on the line below.

1_____10

(Not at all)   (Exhausted)

Explain your answer below. If you need more rest, note the things that are causing you to be tired. If you are feeling rested, list some specific reasons you are doing so well—and refer to this list when life gets busy in the future!

How often do you observe a weekly Sabbath—a day of the week when you stop your regular work and remember God and God's good gifts?

__ Always __ Usually __Sometimes __ Rarely __ Never

If you struggle to take a Sabbath rest, what are some of the barriers that prevent you from ceasing your regular work (including errands) one day a week?

Sometimes we try to rest but get interrupted. And other times our "rest" really isn't rest at all. Because I work in ministry, I've taken Friday as my day off for almost fifteen years. However, for at least ten of those years, I treated Friday as my "catch-up" day. It was my day for laundry, cleaning, errands, and coffee or lunch with friends. By Friday evening, I was often more tired than I am at the end of a regular workday.

A few years ago, I had to prepare a teaching on Sabbath, and I felt a strong conviction to really lean into God's example in Genesis 2:3. Though I thought that I was honoring the Sabbath by not going into the office on my day off, I realized that I still was "working." So, in the past few years I've disciplined myself not to work on my Sabbath day. This can create tension at times when I'm feeling the pressure of deadlines or thinking about e-mails I received on Thursday evening. However, I do not want the urgent to hijack my heart and mind from attending to the important. I must have the discipline to know when I must stop *doing* and focus on just *being* so that I can refocus my identity on who God has created me to be.

Sabbath is about learning how to "be" and breaking away from the rhythm of "doing." It's a spiritual principle that calls us to learn how to trust in God instead of believing that everything depends on our own efforts.

Though God gave the Israelites simple instructions for rest in Exodus 20, the religious leaders in Jesus' time turned the Sabbath into a bunch of rules. Instead of a day defined by resting in God's provision, the people had many obligations to satisfy. Jesus pushed back against the rules that negated the blessing of the Sabbath.

Read Mark 2:27 in the margin. What did Jesus mean by this?

One of the key principles behind the Sabbath is trusting God to be God while we care for our bodies. Friends, we can run that errand or return that e-mail, but taking care of that "one" thing will cost us the blessing that God wants to give us: rest. Rest blesses us.

Let's consider three ways that rest blesses us.

1. Rest gives us a break from work and everyday concerns.

When we take a holy day of rest, we take our hands off our work and leave it in God's hands. There always will be one more thing calling for my attention, yet I remember Jesus' words when reflecting on Mary's choice to sit and listen at His feet: "There is only one thing worth being concerned about. Mary has discovered it, and it will not be taken away from her" (Luke 10:42).

Then Jesus said to them, "The Sabbath was made to meet the needs of people, and not people to meet the requirements of the Sabbath." (Mark 2:27)

Taking a day of rest is not as simple to do as it sounds, but it is a faith-building experience! I challenge you to do this. On your chosen day, pray and ask for God's help. If you don't have words for that prayer, you can use these:

Dear God, today is a holy day of rest dedicated to You. There is so much that needs to be done, but I choose to trust in Your timing and provision. If there are gaps that need to be filled today in my life, I trust You to fill them. Help me not to worry about what isn't getting done but to trust in Your love and care for all that concerns me, including my body. Today I will keep my focus on You. Amen.

2. Rest reconnects us to God.

In Mark 12:30, Jesus reminds us that the sole purpose of our lives is to love God with all that we are—our hearts, minds, bodies, and souls. Though we are to love God in this way every day, we can easily become distracted if we are constantly devoting our time and energy in other areas. To keep this purpose central in our lives, we must take time to rest and reconnect with God.

When we engage in a holy day of rest, we intentionally set our focus on God, finding ways to connect to God with our hearts, minds, bodies, and souls throughout that day. We can do this by praying, reading or studying the Bible, listening to worship songs, worshiping God (corporately or privately), enjoying God's creation, or even just taking a nap!

In 1 Kings 19, we see that the prophet Elijah was suffering through a very difficult time in his life. After a series of high and low points, he was exhausted by life. In fact, he questioned whether or not he should have been born. God sent an angel to feed Elijah and told him to take a nap, too. When we neglect our physical bodies, our spiritual sensors are impacted as well. After food and sleep, Elijah rallied and traveled to Mount Sinai. There, Elijah connected with God in a powerful way before God sent him along for his next assignment.

Sometimes a nap is the most spiritual thing we can do!

What are your favorite ways to reconnect with God?

3. Rest revives our resources.

Think about Psalm 23 for a moment. God is our shepherd, our caregiver, and our provider. I love the psalmist's description of how God takes care of us: "He lets me rest in green meadows" and "He renews my strength" (23:2a, 3a). Notice how this chapter opens with attention focused on how God cares for us—and we don't have to do a thing for it!

There are times when we need an extended time of rest—like a vacation! God gives vacations a "thumbs up." However, vacation isn't about *where* but *when*. We don't need to go to a five-star resort or book an expensive cruise or even get out of town. Vacation is about an extended time away from our regular rhythm of life.

If you don't think you can afford to take a break in your week, or if you aren't sure how you can afford a vacation, I encourage you to be like the little boy with five loaves of bread and two fish in Mark 6. That little boy took what he had and offered it to Jesus, who blessed it so that there was more than enough. Take what you have and give it to Jesus, and He will provide a way!

Remembering that God cares for you enables you to cease from *doing* all of the time and attend to just *being* in God's presence. Resting in God's presence will fill your heart, restore your soul, and renew your strength. Won't you rest in God today?

Live It Out

1. **What is one thing that God impressed upon your heart during today's study?**

2. **What do you sense God leading you to think or do differently as a result of what you've studied?**

Talk with God

God wants to bless you through rest! There is no substitute for rest, and that is why God instructs us to regularly set aside a holy day for rest. If you are struggling with how to integrate a regular rhythm of rest into your life, then that is what you should pray about today. Listen specifically for God's whispers about why He needs you to rest.

> "And you must love the LORD your God with all your heart, all your soul, all your mind, and all your strength." (Mark 12:30)

Day 4: Becoming a Woman Who CARES—Exercise and Smile

Beauty Mark

Exercising and smiling allow us to serve others and honor God.

Beauty Regimen

The final two words in the acronym CARES stand for exercise and smile. While grinning comes naturally to me, I can't say the same about exercise. I've always been an athlete, but I'd be lying if I told you that I love to work out. I don't. But I do it anyway.

For some of you, working out is much easier than smiling. In fact, smiling is stressful for some of you. When you smile, you feel like you're expressing more of yourself than is comfortable, so you reserve your smiles for very specific situations or conditions.

As I prepared to write today's lesson, I struggled with how to connect these two concepts. But after a bit of study, I came across a word that links them together beautifully: endorphins.

Our bodies release endorphins when we exercise. Endorphins are chemicals that trigger a positive feeling in our bodies. And positive feelings result in smiles. I love that God created our bodies to release a "feel-good" hormone when we do something good for our bodies!

If you are a runner, you know all about endorphins, which produce a feeling called a "runner's high." I've never actually experienced that feeling when I run. I think I got close a few weeks ago, but it was probably just relief from the feeling that I wasn't going to die on the sidewalk!

Endorphins are produced in the brain, spinal cord, and other parts of the body and then released in response to neurotransmitters, which are chemicals in the brain. The release of endorphins acts an as a nonaddictive pain reliever and sedative, lowering our stress and anxiety as well as boosting our self-esteem and sleep.[13]

In a nutshell, endorphins help us smile more, and smiling has been scientifically proven to be a good thing!

Today we're going to explore why God created our bodies to need regular movement and the purpose of smiling. Let's have some fun with this!

Exercise

Like the topic of food, so much has been written about exercise. I'm not a fitness expert, so we're not going to talk about specific kinds of exercise. Instead we're going to focus on why we need to develop strong, fit bodies.

Read Ephesians 2:10 in the margin. Underline the word *masterpiece* **(some translations use the word** *workmanship***). Why are we God's masterpiece?**

For we are God's masterpiece. He has created us anew in Christ Jesus, so we can do the good things he planned for us long ago. (Ephesians 2:10)

What does God want us to do?

When we think of priceless artwork, we think of those pieces that are carefully guarded or locked away in a museum. However, as God's masterpiece, we are intended to be put on a roadshow! The phrase "good things" (some translations say "good works") isn't related to earning our salvation or remaining in good standing with God. Jesus Christ paid all of sin debt. Rather, this phrase refers to the fruit or outcome of our faith. God has plans for us to make an impact in this world. If His plan is for us to share the gospel message and do His kingdom work, then we must take care of our bodies to the best of our abilities so that we can carry out that work. Of course, some of us have health conditions that are beyond our control. Some of us are battling autoimmune diseases, fibromyalgia, cancer, or other conditions that impact our health and limit our physical abilities. But doing whatever we can do to take care of our bodies helps each of us to give all that we can for God's purposes in our lives and our world. Even when we are limited physically, we can use our bodies to the best of our abilities for the glory of God.

While I realize this topic may be uncomfortable for some, I believe it is a valuable dialogue. Stay with me as we take an honest inventory. If you have physical limitations or challenges *beyond your control*, consider the highest level of health possible for you in light of your condition or circumstances.

How would you describe your current physical condition?

What are the areas where you need improvement?

Are you making any excuses? What is keeping you from striving for the highest level of health that you can attain?

Have you declined any ministry opportunities because of your health (excluding physical conditions beyond your control)?

What physical fitness goals do you have?

How might reaching these goals impact the ways you serve God?

As Christian women, we have the best reason of all to be healthy and fit: the gospel! Even though I don't love to exercise, that's my reason for staying fit—so I can give my all to sharing the message of God's love and serving others in the name of Jesus Christ.

I love going on mission trips! I've taken eight trips overseas. On some of those trips I'm out building houses, and during others I'm speaking at women's conferences. Early on I realized that my stamina was connected to my overall level of fitness. In order to serve the needs of those I go to serve, I have to remain fit. When we're meeting the needs of others, our bodies are working harder than usual. In fact, I tend to increase my workouts before going on mission trips to make sure that I am as fit and healthy as I can be.

I also believe that God has called each of us to use our gifts and talents within the local church. At my church, there are all sorts of things I can do to help people connect with God. There are service opportunities for people regardless of their age or stage in life. No doubt you have similar opportunities at your local church. Even if you are managing physical conditions that are beyond your control, God still has work for you to do— meaningful work that will make a difference!

In 1 Corinthians 6, Paul instructs the Corinthian Christians to avoid using their bodies for sexual immorality. Even as Paul instructs them about the sin of sexual immorality, he casts an even greater vision for the purpose of our bodies.

Read 1 Corinthians 6:19-20 in the margin. How are our bodies described?

[19]Don't you realize that your **body** is the temple of the Holy Spirit, who lives in you and was given to you by God? You do not belong to yourself, [20]for God bought you with a high price. So you must honor God with your body. (1 Corinthians 6:19-20, *emphasis added*)

How does caring for our physical bodies honor God?

It should make sense that if our bodies are designed for God's use, then He would have specific purposes for us to use our bodies to accomplish. Even if you have limited physical capacity, God can still work in you and through you!

For most of us, exercise can be a struggle. According to a 2014 National Health Interview Survey, slightly less than 50 percent of women aged twenty-five to sixty-four met federally established guidelines for aerobic exercise, and slightly more than 50 percent of women aged eighteen to twenty-four met those guidelines.

So why are only roughly 50 percent of women exercising? Though busy schedules and other excuses often keep us from exercising, according to numerous articles online, many of us are afraid of what people will think of us while we exercise. Can you relate? How can we create some simple next steps to honor God by doing what we can to be physically healthy?

Pastor Craig Groeschel leads one of the largest churches in America. However, two decades ago his ministry almost collapsed. The church leaders asked him to do two things: work out and go to counseling to deal with his work-a-holic tendencies. At first, he balked at the church leaders, saying, "I don't have time to work out." Their reply: "You don't have time not to work out."[14]

Sisters, please understand my heart. I'm not instructing you about *how* to exercise. My purpose is simply to cast a vision for *why* you should exercise on a regular basis. If you aren't sure where to start, perhaps these practical tips from Pastor Groeschel will help:

1. Decide to start.
2. Decide to stop [the behaviors, mindsets, and attitudes that hinder you].
3. Decide to stay [the course].
4. Decide to go [and take a step of faith].[15]

How could applying these principles in the area of exercise change how you serve God and others?

Imagine what could happen if we were fit and ready for God to call us and use us anytime or anywhere in the world. When we take the time to care for our bodies, it doesn't matter if God calls us to rock babies in the church nursery, read a book to a preschooler, answer phones or prepare a mailing, pray with someone, teach a class or study, volunteer for a high school retreat, go on a mission trip, or do a myriad of other things—we can be ready for anything!

Smiling

In his TED Talk "The Hidden Power of Smiling," presenter Ron Gutman explains how smiling impacts our society. After showing that smiling is a universal form of communication, he presents some interesting facts:

- More than a third of us smile more than twenty times per day.
- Less than 14 percent of us smile only five times per day.
- Children smile as much as four hundred times per day.[16]

Which group describes you?

Gutman goes on to explain how smiling is both powerful and satisfying. He captures my attention when he notes that smiling stimulates our reward center in a way that chocolate cannot match. According to Gutman, British researchers discovered that one smile can generate the same level of brain stimulation as up to two thousand bars of chocolate! Here are some other benefits of smiling that Gutman names:

1. Smiling can make us healthier.
2. Smiling reduces cortisol, a stress-enhancing hormone, and can reduce blood pressure.
3. Smiling makes us look good in the eyes of others.
4. When we smile, we are more courteous and likable and perceived as being more competent. [17]

I don't know about you, but that just makes me want to smile!

Do you remember the song, "If You're Happy and You Know It"? It reminds us that if we're happy, our faces "will surely show it." That cheerful song has been sung by millions of little kids in Sunday school. Even for us adults, that simple song can be a reminder that we serve a loving God who cares for us on the inside and out.

But how often do our faces smile and glow with thankfulness for God's love and care toward us? Sadly, not as often as they should.

What do the following verses tell us about the impact that happiness and gratitude have in our lives?

Proverbs 15:13

Proverbs 15:30

Proverbs 17:22

Despite both the physiological and scriptural reasons for smiling, at times we can find it difficult to smile. Even though I know that God is always with me, there are times when my smile is lost behind my struggles. The expectation isn't that we'll always be smiling; rather, our focus should be to allow the joy of the Lord to fuel our hearts and minds. When that happens, a smile is always waiting in the wings, even if that smile is preceded by tears or hardship.

In those times when you've found yourself struggling to smile, what have been some of the common reasons for your struggle? List a couple below:

Now put a checkmark beside those reasons that you can do something about and would like to challenge or eliminate. Write a comment beside each one, noting what you might do.

Whether smiling doesn't come naturally to you, you're out of practice, or you simply want to smile even more, here are some practical tips that you can try:

- Whenever you look into a mirror, smile at yourself. You deserve to experience the beauty of your own smile.
- Maintaining an attitude of gratitude is a guaranteed smile builder. Whether you write out a daily list or mentally keep track, make sure to list everything in your life that blesses you on a regular basis.

- Smile at everyone you see. Trust me, you'll bless untold multitudes of people in this way.

What other ideas can you add to the list?

On a serious note, one of the reasons why this section is at the end of our study is because our ugly struggle with beauty can make smiling difficult. By this point, I pray that God has worked through this study in tremendous ways in your life and you've discovered lots about which to smile at yourself and others. However, if you're still struggling to lift yourself out of a dark place, then I want to encourage you to speak to a trusted Christian friend or pastor—or perhaps a licensed professional counselor or physician. You may be dealing with a medical issue and need professional or medical assistance.

While smiling doesn't seem like a hard-hitting spiritual topic, it's one gift that you can share with everyone you meet. Your smile is powerful. Your smile can transform someone's day. Never underestimate what God can do through you when you lift the corners of your mouth and share a smile with someone who needs it.

Live It Out

1. **What is one thing that God impressed upon your heart during today's study?**

2. **What do you sense God leading you to think or do differently as a result of what you've studied?**

Talk with God

Did you sense God's whispers at any point during today's study? If so, talk with Him about what you sensed. It's hard starting any new behaviors such as exercising or smiling more, but I pray that you will allow God to plant a new conviction deep inside your heart and mind. Commit to allowing God to grow that conviction within you so that your body and your smile can open doors for the message of the gospel to flow through you into the lives of those God places in your path.

Day 5: Balanced Beauty

Beauty Mark

Allowing our inner beauty and outer beauty to shine at the right times gives us the influence and impact to change the world for Christ.

Beauty Regimen

On our last day of study together, we're going to look again at the story of my favorite woman in the Bible: Because she demonstrates what can happen when a woman leverages her inner and physical beauty in correct proportion, her story deserves a closer look. As we saw in Week 3, God used Esther's inner and physical beauty to save the lives of His chosen people, the Israelites. Her story demonstrates how God's purpose unfolds behind the scenes in all of our lives as He works all things out for His ultimate good.

Esther's story began when the king sent his people into the city of Susa, located in Persia, to bring him young women so that he could select a new queen. Esther was one of the women selected, and early on she made an impression.

Read Esther 2:8-9. Who noticed Esther, and how did he take special care of her?

As the man in charge of this group of women, Hegai was there to accomplish a goal: prepare the women to meet the king. No doubt King Ahasuerus expected near perfection for his next queen, so Hegai looked for a woman possessing not only great physical beauty but also inner beauty.

Read Esther 2:12. Why types of physical preparations did the ladies undergo and for how long?

Recall an instance when you spent a lot of time preparing yourself for a special event or occasion. How much time did you spend preparing, and why did you take extra time and attention for that special event?

We might be shocked at the lengths that celebrities employ to look glamorous, but many of their strategies would be considered elementary compared to what Esther and the other candidates experienced. I don't know about you, but I think that after twelve months of daily spa treatments and the best foods, I'd probably look pretty good!

While Esther's body was attended to for months on end, she still had to manage her inner life. If you've read Esther's story, you know that she was orphaned and taken in by her cousin, Mordecai. He told Esther to keep her Jewish identity a secret while living in the palace. If you've studied world history, you also know that King Ahasuerus (Xerxes) had a reputation as a brutal man. So Esther had a lot to think about during those long months of pampering.

Read Esther 2:15. How did Esther demonstrate gentleness (humility) and wisdom?

It could have been so different! As potential queens, the women had access to endless wardrobes and jewelry intended to bolster their self-image and impress the king. Yet Esther possessed humility and wisdom by asking for counsel on what to wear.

In the end, Esther became queen. Her story could have ended there, but an evil plan was revealed after Esther was crowned queen. However, God's plan to save the Jewish people was already in place.

Read Esther 3:1-6. Who hatched a plan to eliminate the Jews?

Esther's cousin, Mordecai, discovered Haman's evil plan and notified Esther. At first, she was disinterested in helping until Mordecai sent her a note with a reality check attached.

Read Esther 4:1-17.

What was the message that Mordecai sent to Esther about what would happen if she did nothing to help? (vv. 13-14)

What was the question that Mordecai asked Esther? (v. 14)

Esther's physical beauty wasn't going to save her life.

If we put all of our effort into pursuing physical beauty, we aren't going to have what it takes when the pressure builds up in our lives. When tragedy strikes or when relationships run off course, long eyelashes and the perfect outfit don't mean a thing. A woman whose mind is preoccupied with physical beauty will collapse under the strain.

Inner beauty gives us the courage to walk with conviction instead of giving ourselves over to what feels right in the moment or reacting out of fear. Inner beauty explains the decision to display kindness rather than anger or the decision to display humility when snarkiness or disrespectfulness might feel better in the moment.

Esther girded herself for an unplanned and potentially deadly encounter with the king. In the face of uncertainty, she accepted whatever might happen while attempting to save her people's lives.

What was Esther's response to Mordecai? (v. 16)

On the day she appeared before the king, Esther put on her best clothing and robes. While she may have been distraught over the situation, she still understood the value of preparing her outer self for the task at hand. It brings to mind that old saying: "If you look better, you'll feel better."

If the king was attracted only to Esther's physical features, she probably would have been killed for approaching unannounced. There were lots of beautiful women hanging around the palace, and any one of them could have assumed the queen's crown. But that's not what happened.

So why didn't the king kill Esther? It goes without saying that the providence of God was at work. But could it also be due in part to the fact that the king was attracted to Esther's inner beauty? I think so.

Read Esther 5:4. When Esther appeared before the king, what was her request?

What kind of demeanor did she express while making this request?

While Esther displayed qualities that we'd associate with a gentle and quiet spirit, she also had to fight through fear and demonstrate courage because the lives of the entire Jewish race were at risk. Esther shows us that strength and beauty complement each other perfectly.

There was a God-ordained event that took place after Esther, King Ahasuerus, and Haman had dinner together. In a twist of events, the king ordered Haman to show honor to Mordecai in the streets of the city. Then Haman met the king and queen for dinner once again. This time, Esther told the king what Haman was planning.

Read Esther 7:1-7. What type of attitude did Esther's words convey? (v. 3)

The next few chapters tell us that Esther went to the king to plead for a countermeasure to save her people from slaughter. The king agreed, and Esther fulfilled her mission.

I love Esther's story for so many reasons. While God's name isn't mentioned in the book of Esther, His sovereignty is undisputed. I also love that God uses a beautiful woman to play a crucial role in His divine plan. Esther wasn't just a pretty face but a woman of courage and conviction.

Truth is, I want to be like Esther. Though I enjoy clothes and fashion, I always want to be a woman used by God to have an impact in the world around me. I hope that you feel that way too.

This is why I am so thankful that you embarked on the *Beautiful Already* journey. We were created to have an impact in our world. But for too many of us, our influence and impact are being hindered by our ugly struggle with beauty and our poor self-image. My prayer is that God has brought you to a new place of knowledge and understanding. I hope that you've discovered that you can love yourself on the inside *and* out because that is how God loves you. Most of all, I pray you will never forget that you are beautiful already because God created you!

Live It Out

1. **What is one thing that God impressed upon your heart during today's study?**

2. What do you sense God leading you to think or do differently as a result of what you've studied?

3. Did you have an "aha" moment or two during the course of this study? What were some new perspectives that you gained about God's truth as it pertains to your ugly struggle with beauty?

4. What portions of your ugly struggle with beauty are you ready to leave behind as a result of this study? How have you been able to deal with any beauty-related shame or self-esteem issues?

5. Everything is a process and we all move forward at different rates. It's OK if you still need more time to overcome your struggles. Are there areas that you still need to work on or guard your heart against?

6. Moving forward, what excites you about the future?

Talk with God

Take a deep breath and smile! You've taken such an important journey, and now is a wonderful time to give thanks for this opportunity. As you pray, thank God for the places where you've overcome struggles and ask God to guide you toward healing for any remaining struggles. After you pray, take a moment and sit silently. Listen for any leadings from God about next steps that you should take, whether joining a new women's Bible study or talking with a trusted Christian friend about this experience.

VIDEO VIEWER GUIDE: WEEK 6

DISCOVERING YOUR BEAUTY BALANCE

When it comes to beauty, it's not a _____ proposition.

What's on the inside does matter _____, but it's not the only thing that _____.

> **C** lothes/Appearance
> **A** ppetite
> **R** est
> **E** xercise
> **S** mile

One of my favorite sayings is, "Don't wear clothes that make you _____."

A hunger that is not _____ is a hunger that will _____ us.

Setting aside one day a week to rest is learning how to _____ instead of learning how to _____.

For we are God's masterpiece. He has created us anew in Christ Jesus, so we can do the good things he planned for us long ago. (Ephesians 2:10)

We can do the best with what God has given us by being as _____ as we can be.

There is something _____ that happens when we smile.

VIDEO VIEWER GUIDE: WEEK 6

We live in the beauty balance, and for each of us, the proportion is going to be unique.

Esther's outer beauty is what garnered the king's _____.

Inner beauty is what she used to gain his _____.

We celebrate Esther because she shows us what it means to be a beautiful woman on

the _____ and _____.

She is clothed with strength and dignity,
*   and she laughs without fear of the future.*
When she speaks, her words are wise,
*   and she gives instructions with kindness.*
*   (Proverbs 31:25-26)*

NOTES

Week 1: All Aboard the Struggle Bus

1. "Commentary on Genesis 2:25," *Bible Hub*, accessed August 27, 2015, http://biblehub.com/commentaries/genesis/2-25.htm.
2. "20 Facts About Eye Color and Blinking," *Discovery Eye Foundation*, July 15, 2014, https://discoveryeye.org/blog/20-facts-eye-color-and-blinking/.
3. "Difference Between Eyesight and Vision," *Differencebetween.com*, November 6, 2012, http://www.differencebetween.com/difference-between-eyesight-and-vs-vision/.
4. "Celebrities Talk Beauty," *Harper's Bazaar*, June 18, 2010, www.harpersbazaar.com/beauty/makeup-articles/celebrity-beauty-0610#slide2.
5. "Origin of the Name Barbara," *Baby Name Wizard*, accessed August 28, 2015, http://www.babynamewizard.com/baby-name/girl/barbara.
6. *Urban Dictionary*, s.v. "Barbara," last modified April 8, 2007, http://www.urbandictionary.com/define.php?term=Barbara.
7. *Ellicot's Commentary for English Readers*, s.v. "Genesis 29:11," accessed August 31, 2015, http://biblehub.com/commentaries/genesis/29-17.htm.
8. See Barbara L. Roose, *Enough Already*, (Nashville: Abingdon Press, 2015), 129–30.
9. Carol Ross Joynt, "What It's Like Protecting the President: Former Secret Service Agent Dan Bongino Tells His Tale," *Washingtonian*, December 4, 2014, http://www.washingtonian.com/blogs/capitalcomment/what-its-like-protecting-the-president-former-secret-service-agent-dan-bongino-tells-his-tale.php.
10. *MacLaren's Expositions*, s.v. "Proverbs 4:23," accessed August 31, 2015, http://biblehub.com/commentaries/proverbs/4-23.htm.
11. *Strong's Concordance*, s.v. "Sulagógeó," accessed August 31, 2015, http://biblehub.com/greek/4812.htm.

Week 2: Defining Divine Beauty

1. Crispin Sartwell, *Stanford Encyclopedia of Philosophy*, s.v. "Beauty," last modified September 4, 2012, http://plato.stanford.edu/entries/beauty/.
2. Ashly Perez, "This Woman Had Her Face Photoshopped in Over 25 Countries to Examine Global Beauty Standards, *BuzzFeed Life*, June 25, 2014, http://www.buzzfeed.com/ashleyperez/global-beauty-standards#.yrWbkZV08.
3. Ibid.

4. Esther Honig, "Before and After," accessed September 1, 2015, http://www.estherhonig .com/#!commercial/cpax.

5. R. C. Sproul, *The Holiness of God: Revised and Expanded*, 2nd ed. (Carol Stream, Ill.: Tyndale House, 1998), 200.

6. See R. C. Sproul, "Our Beautiful God," *Ligonier Ministries*, December 1, 2014, http://www .ligonier.org/learn/articles/for-glory-and-beauty/.

7. Bill Bright, "Truth Really Matters," accessed September 2, 2015, http://www.cru.org/train-and -grow/devotional-life/discover-god/god-is-absolute-truth.6.html.

8. Augustine of Hippo in "Quotes on the Goodness and Mercy of God," *Bible Hub*, accessed September 2, 2015, http://biblehub.com/library/augustine/writings_in_connection_with _the_manichaean_controversy_/chapter_1_name_the_highest.htm.

9. Arthur W. Pink, "The Attributes of God," *Providence Baptist Ministries*, accessed September 2, 2015, http://www.pbministries.org/books/pink/Attributes/attrib_11.htm.

10. John Piper, "What Is God's Glory?" *Desiring God*, July 22, 2014, http://www.desiringgod.org /interviews/what-is-god-s-glory.

11. John Piper, "How Pervasive and Practical Is the Beauty of God?" *Desiring God*, July 7, 2013, http://www.desiringgod.org/articles/how-pervasive-and-practical-is-the-beauty-of-god.

12. *Strong's Concordance*, s.v. "Hagios," accessed September 3, 2015, http://biblehub.com /greek/40.htm.

13. James Bryan Smith, *Good and Beautiful God* (Downers Grove, Ill.: InterVarsity Press, 2009), 122–23.

14. Jerry Bridges, *The Pursuit of Holiness: 25th Anniversary Edition* (Colorado Springs, Col.: NavPress, 2003), 32.

15. Nathalie Alonso, "7 Natural Wonders of the World Today," *USA Today*, accessed September 3, 2015, http://traveltips.usatoday.com/7-natural-wonders-world-today-101007.html.

16. *Strong's Concordance*, s.v. "Towb," accessed September 4, 2015, http://biblehub.com /hebrew/2896.htm.

17. Sproul, *The Holiness of God: Revised and Expanded*, 163–164.

Week 3: Celebrating What We See

1. Robin Roberts for ABC News, "The Mirror-Free Bride," *20/20* video, 6:42, accessed September 9, 2015, http://abcnews.go.com/2020/video/mirror-free-bride-17016401.

2. Ibid.

3. Taken from *Snow White and the Seven Dwarfs*, Walt Disney Pictures, accessed September 9, 2015, http://www.imdb.com/title/tt0029583/quotes.

4. Heather Turgeon, "Do Babies Recognize Themselves in the Mirror?" *Parenting*, accessed September 10, 2015, http://www.momtastic.com/parenting/101560-do-babies-recognize -themselves-in-the-mirror/.

5. *Strong's Concordance*, s.v. "Zeteo," accessed September 10, 2015, http://biblehub.com/greek /2212.htm.

6. Karri, "The Mirror," May 8, 2015, https://thegreatbattleblog.wordpress.com/2015/05/08/the -mirror/.

7. "Lizzie Velasquez, Born Without Adipose Tissues: 'Maybe You Should Stop Staring And Start Learning,'" *Huffpost Healthy Living*, October 2, 2015, http://www.huffingtonpost.com/2012 /09/13/lizzie-velasquez-adipose-tissue-neonatal-progeroid-syndrome_n_1880875.html.

8. "Bullied Girl Voted the Ugliest on the Internet Gives an Amazing Speech," YouTube video, 10:20, July 18, 2013, https://www.youtube.com/watch?v=R0OV92Yyl20.

9. Ibid.

10. Ibid.

11. "Human Body Facts," *Science Kids*, accessed September 11, 2015, http://www.sciencekids.co.nz /sciencefacts/humanbody.html.

12. Tony Evans, "Are Black People Cursed? The Curse of Ham," *Eternal Perspective Ministries*, January 18, 2010, http://www.epm.org/resources/2010/Jan/18/are-black-people-cursed-curse-ham/.

Week 4: Gentle and Quiet Beauty

1. *Oxford Dictionaries*, s.v."Submission," accessed September 16, 2015, http://www.oxforddictionaries .com/definition/english/submission.

2. Whit Bronaugh, "Dyerville Giant," accessed September 16, 2015, http://www.caforestsoils.org/paul -zinke/zinke-storytelling/dyerville-giant/; and Humboldt County Convention and Visitor's Bureau, "Founder's Grove and The Dyerville Giant," accessed September 16, 2015, http://redwoods.info /showrecord.asp?id=1710.

3. *Merriam-Webster 11th Collegiate Dictionary*, s.v. "Taproot," accessed September 17, 2015, http://www .merriam-webster.com/dictionary/taproot.

Week 5: Winning Our Ugly Struggle

1. Madelyn Chung, "Essena O'Neill, Instagram Celebrity, Deletes Account, Reveals Truth Behind Posts," *The Huffington Post*, modified November 11, 2015, http://www.huffingtonpost.ca/2015/11/02/essena -oneill-social-media-is-not-real-life_n_8455278.html.

2. Maria Popova "The Nature of the Self," *Daily Good*, March 13, 2014, http://www.dailygood.org /story/665/the-nature-of-the-self-maria-popova/.

3. Rick Warren, "Embrace Your Identity in Christ," *Daily Hope with Rick Warren*, May 21, 2014, http://rickwarren.org/devotional/english/embrace-your-identity-in-christ.

4. "History of Feminine Hygiene Products," *Menstral Cup*, accessed November 17, 2015, http://menstrualcup.co/history-menstrual-products/.

5. "Cosmetic Procedures: Scars," *WebMD*, accessed November 17, 2015, http://www.webmd.com/beauty/skin/cosmetic-procedures-scars?page=1.

6. "What Is Scar Revision Surgery?" *American Society of Plastic Surgeons*, accessed November 17, 2015, http://www.plasticsurgery.org/reconstructive-procedures/scar-revision.html.

7. For details about the crucifixion, see Matt Slick, "The Crucifixion of Jesus," *Christian Apologetics and Research Ministry*, accessed November 17, 2015, https://carm.org/christianity/miscellaneous-topics /crucifixion-jesus.

8. Mandisa, "What Scars Are For," accessed November 17, 2015 , www.metrolyrics.com/what-scars-are -for-lyrics-mandisa.html.

9. C. Bushdid, M. O. Magnasco, L. B. Vosshall, and A. Keller, "Humans Can Discriminate More than 1 Trillion Olfactory Stimuli," *Science* 343, no. 6177 (March 21, 2014): 1370–72, http://www.sciencemag.org /content/343/6177/1370 (accessed November 21, 2015).

10. Sarah Dowdey, "How Smell Works," *HowStuffWorks*, accessed November 17, 2015, http://health .howstuffworks.com/mental-health/human-nature/perception/smell3.htm.

11. *Dictionary of Bible Themes*, s.v. "Smell," accessed November 17, 2015, https://www.biblegateway.com /resources/dictionary-of-bible-themes/5183-smell.

12. UNRV, s.v., "Roman Triumph," *United Nations of Roma Victrix,* accessed November 17, 2015, http://www.unrv.com/culture/roman-triumph.php.

13. "Footnote b," accessed November 17, 2015, https://www.biblegateway compassage/?search =Mark+14&version=NLT.

14. Vince DiPasquale, "The Four Seasons of Life," *StartingPoint*, accessed November 17, 2015, http://startingpoint.org/the-four-seasons-of-life/.

Week 6: Discovering Your Beauty Balance

1. *Merriam-Webster 11th Collegiate Dictionary*, s.v., "Dignity," accessed November 17, 2015, http://www.merriam-webster.com/dictionary/dignity.

2. "Proverbs 11:22," accessed November 17, 2015, http://www.biblestudytools.com /commentaries/gills-exposition-of-the-bible/proverbs-11-22.html.

3. John Piper, "A Woman Who Fears the Lord Is to Be Praised," *Desiring God*, May 10, 1981, http://www.desiringgod.org/messages/a-woman-who-fears-the-lord-is-to-be-praised.

4. "What Is Appetite?" *Appecal*, accessed November 17, 2015, http://www.myappecal.com/what -is-appetite.htm.

5. Leila Gerstein and Carter Covington, "Take Me Home, Country Roads," *Hart of Dixie*, season 2, episode 14, directed by Jeremiah Chechik, aired February 5, 2013, the CW Television Network.

6. "Jacob's name is Israel. So why is he called Jacob?" *Biblical Hermeneutics Stack Exchange*, accessed November 17, 2015, http://hermeneutics.stackexchange.com/questions/952/jacobs -name-is-israel-so-why-is-he-still-called-jacob.

7. R. C. Sproul, "A Despised Birthright," *Ligonier Ministries*, accessed November 17, 2015, http://www.ligonier.org/learn/devotionals/despised-birthright/.

8. Samantha Lauria, "H.A.L.T.—Hungry, Angry, Lonely, Tired," *First Step to Freedom*, accessed November 17, 2015, http://www.addiction-recovery.com/HALT-hungry-angry-lonely -tired.php.

9. "Economics: Whatever Happened to Keynes' 15-hour Working Week?" *The Guardian*, August 31, 2008, http://www.theguardian.com/business/2008/sep/01/economics.

10. Barbara Roose, Facebook post, August 12, 2015, https://www.facebook.com/barbara.roose /posts/10207569689387397.

11. "Commentary on Genesis 2:1-3," *Matthew Henry's Concise Commentary*, accessed November 17, 2015, http://biblehub.com/genesis/2-2.htm.

12. *Baker's Evangelical Dictionary of Biblical Theology*, s.v. "Sabbath," accessed November 17, 2015, http://www.biblestudytools.com/dictionary/sabbath/.

13. "Exercise and Depression," *WebMD*, http://www.webmd.com/depression/guide/exercise -depression (accessed November 17, 2015).

14. Craig Groeschel, "My Story: I Decided to Start," Message Transcript, LifeChurch.tv. See also http://www.life.churc/watch/my-story/ (accessed November 17, 2015).

15. Ibid.

16. Ron Gutman, "The Hidden Power of Smiling," *Ted Conferences*, March 2011, https://www.ted .com/talks/ron_gutman_the_hidden_power_of_smiling?language=en#t-411011.

17. Ibid.

18. Jose Luis Gonzalez-Balado, *Mother Teresa: In My Own Words* (Liguori, Mo.: Liguori, 1997), 38.

MY BEAUTY NARRATIVE

_____

_____

_____

_____

_____

_____

_____

_____

_____

_____

_____

_____

_____

_____

_____

_____

_____

_____

_____

_____

_____

_____

_____

_____

_____

_____

_____

_____

_____

_____

_____

_____

_____

_____

_____

_____

MY BEAUTY NARRATIVE

Jessica LaGrone is Dean of the Chapel at Asbury Theological Seminary and an acclaimed pastor, teacher, and speaker who enjoys leading retreats and events throughout the United States. She previously served as Pastor of Creative Ministries at The Woodlands UMC in Houston, Texas. She is the author of _Namesake: When God Rewrites Your Story, Broken and Blessed: How God Changed the World Through One Imperfect Family,_ and _Set Apart: Holy Habits of Prophets and Kings._ She and her husband, Jim, have two young children. For speaking and booking information and to follow her blog, Reverend Mother, visit JessicaLagrone.com.

Babbie Mason is an award-winning singer and songwriter; a women's conference speaker; a leader of worship celebration-concerts for women; adjunct professor of songwriting at Lee University; and television talk-show host of _Babbie's House._ She has led worship for national and international events hosted by Billy Graham, Charles Stanley, Anne Graham Lotz, Women of Faith, and others. She is the author of _Embraced by God_ and _This I Know for Sure._ For information about speaking and events, visit Babbie.com.

Barbara L. Roose is a popular speaker and author who is passionate about connecting women to one another and to God. Previously Barb was Executive Director of Ministry at CedarCreek Church in Perrysburg, Ohio, where she served on staff for fourteen years and co-led the annual Fabulous Women's Conference. Barb is a frequent speaker at women's conferences and other events. She lives in Toledo, Ohio, with her husband, Matt. They are the proud parents of three beautiful daughters, two dogs, and a grumpy rabbit named Pal. For events and booking information and to follow her blog, visit BarbRoose.com.

Get more information at

Kimberly Dunnam Reisman is known for her effective and engaging preaching and teaching. Kim is the World Director of World Methodist Evangelism and has served as the Executive Director of Next Step Evangelism Ministries and Adjunct Professor at United Theological Seminary. Kim is the author or co-author of numerous books and studies, including *The Christ-Centered Woman: Finding Balance in a World of Extremes*. The mother of three adult children, Kim and her husband live in West Lafayette, Indiana. For information about speaking and events, visit KimberlyReisman.com.

Melissa Spoelstra is a popular women's conference speaker, Bible teacher, and writer who is passionate about helping other women to seek Christ and know Him more intimately through serious Bible study. She is the author of the Bible studies *Jeremiah: Daring to Hope in an Unstable World*, *Joseph: The Journey to Forgiveness*, and *First Corinthians: Living Love When We Disagree* (August 2016). She is also the author of the forthcoming book, *Total Family Makeover*. She lives in Dublin, Ohio, with her pastor husband and four kids. For events and booking information and to follow her blog, visit MelissaSpoelstra.com.

Cindi Wood is a sought-after speaker and Bible teacher with events throughout the United States and abroad. Through biblically-based teaching coupled with humor from daily experience, Cindi offers hope and encouragement to women of all ages and walks of life. She is the author of numerous books and Bible studies, including *Anonymous: Discovering the Somebody You Are to God* and the Frazzled Female series. Cindi lives in Kings Mountain, North Carolina, with her husband, Larry. For events and booking information, visit FrazzledFemale.com.

AbingdonWomen.com.